NELSON

-

POSTCARD HERO

A Trafalgar Bicentennial Tribute

in

200 Picture Postcards

by

Peter Nelson

The Author

Peter Nelson discovered postcards late in life even though he had always had an interest in the past and, particularly, in maritime history. He began collecting Nelson postcards because of the common surname, but then found the man and the story fascinating. Membership of the Nelson Society fed that interest and retirement from his job as a Head Teacher in County Durham, where he was born and grew up, meant that he had, at last, the time to devote to his postcard collecting hobby.

Peter has had articles published regularly by *Picture Postcard Monthly* magazine during the past five years and has developed from that an ever-widening contact group across the world, with whom he regularly corresponds. He is also a member of the Durham Light Infantry Association and two years ago was co-opted to advise on postcard issues and contribute material to *The Durham Bugle*, the magazine published by the Friends of the Durham Light Infantry Museum.

He has been married for 27 years and has two daughters.

This book is dedicated to my brother John who died bravely on Trafalgar Day in 1995.
He would have been proud of that association with one of his heroes.

Published by Reflections of a Bygone Age, Keyworth, Nottingham
(0115-937-4079)
Printed by Adlard Print & Reprographics Ltd, Ruddington

ISBN 1 900138 97 2

CONTENTS

INTRODUCTION

My interest in Nelson and his place in British and World history has been part of my life for as long as I remember. With my surname it was inevitable: my earliest recollections of school include being called Horatio. What might have been even more disconcerting was that my maternal grandmother's maiden name was Hamilton. Yet none of that put me off. The more I learned about the man the more proud I was to have the same name - the surname that is! My respect for Nelson's achievements was tempered over time only by what seemed to be his questionable behaviour in his amorous affairs. As new historical evidence emerged over time, I learned more about Nelson and came to accept him, not so much as a single-minded superman but as a complex, sensitive yet brave individual - very human, in fact, and all the more interesting for it!

Much later in life I developed an interest in collecting picture postcards. I began to collect local topographical cards, and those of places and people, as an embellishment for family history fact sheets but found myself with an embryonic collection of 'Nelson' postcards. I still do not remember when, where or why I collected the first of them, or, indeed, what that postcard was. I have no family history link to the famous Nelson as far as I am aware so can only suppose that at the time it was something to do with the school thing!

In 1995 I joined The Nelson Society* and, apart from discovering that 'Nelson' is still being discovered - in a way still very much alive - I found listed in the Society's Sales items *A Catalogue of Picture Postcards,* which had been produced by David Shannon. I had found a focus and reference for my collecting which was invaluable.

The idea for the book came to me a few years ago, when I looked at the scope of my collection. It occurred to me that the postcards could be used to tell the Nelson story and that they also documented his subsequent impact on national life. Later I realised that the bicentenary of Trafalgar was not too far ahead and I wondered how to present the pictorial history I saw in front of me.

Two hundred years. Could the story be told using 200 postcards? In trying to accomplish that aim, I have tried to include postcards by a representative cross-section of publishers and incorporate examples of those produced by the most well-known. About 70 named publishers featured at the last count! The requirement to tell the story through the postcards has been, however, paramount. Accompanying the postcards there is explanatory text but the postcards, whether artist or photographic in origin, stand on their own. This was always the aim of the quality postcard publishers and the variety of their skill is showcased here. (Further detail to do with Nelson postcards and general collecting advice follows in the *Notes* pages).

I am conscious that Nelson afficionados and postcard collectors are likely to make up the greatest percentage of readers and I hope that this volume not only finds approval with them but also attracts others. If it increases anyone's knowledge of Nelson, or interest in postcard collecting, then that would be a bonus. The book aims to provide a postcard-illustrated timeline and a guide to postcards with a Nelson association. While serving as an introduction to the range of Nelson-related postcards, it should suggest opportunities to would-be collectors for them to explore. For anyone attracted by this challenge, a checklist of known Nelson postcards is included in a separate section.

Horatio Nelson, Trafalgar and *HMS Victory* have, since Nelson's death on 21 October 1805, become embedded in the fabric of the nation and, though only a minority of people may be able to excel in their detailed knowledge of the subject, Nelson is known to all and fascinating to many. Horatio Nelson was, as a warrior, an enigma - thoughtful, kind and caring but also ambitious, ruthless and brave - a charismatic leader who was convinced he had been born to serve God and to fulfil a great purpose.

In the 2003 Annual published by *Picture Postcard Monthly*, the premier magazine for postcard collectors, I wrote an article about the Royal Navy ships named after Nelson. I tried to explain Nelson's place in history thus:

> *Horatio Nelson was described in a TV documentary, shown on 4 March 2002, as the first popular hero or pop idol, as he similarly experienced and enjoyed mass adulation. After his unprecedented victory of the Nile when he totally destroyed the French fleet - no easy push-over - his name was on the lips of every Englishmen, indeed spoken by everyone around the world. He was mobbed wherever he went, showered with gifts and honours, and could have retired honourably considering he had been several times wounded seriously and was in far from pristine condition. Instead he fought on, winning further fame at Copenhagen and then immortality at Trafalgar. The whole nation mourned him and for his funeral procession people turned out in their thousands to show their love and respect.*
>
> *He was such a strong player because he did not simply target victory - he aimed for annihilation of the enemy and the people loved him for his ability to deliver. He was truly extraordinary in that the love and admiration of individuals he did not personally know was matched by the feelings of those who served with him and knew him. There is no higher accolade than to be regarded as the best by your fellow professionals and Nelson was regarded as such by the common sailor as well as by the captain. He was irreplaceable, but his name, at least, could and did live on in the world and particularly the maritime world.*

I hope that this book will encourage an interest and appreciation in Nelson, no matter what form that takes. If it encourages new postcard interest in Nelson then that would be an ideal result. Either way, with its high pictorial content, I should like to think it would appeal to a wide audience and have a small part to play in keeping the 'Immortal Memory' alive.

SeaBritain 2005, launched on Trafalgar Day 2003 by the Duke of Edinburgh, designated the year 2005 as a *Year of the Sea* - a celebration of the place the sea has played in Britain's history. It also celebrated the significant role that Nelson played in winning for Britain a maritime supremacy which lasted over a century - a dominance that permitted British trade to flourish and British influence to spread and strengthen around the world. A programme of events focused on Trafalgar started in June 2005 with a Festival of the Sea at Portsmouth - then the rest of the country was involved, with Trafalgar weekend on 21 - 25 October planned as a finale. The *Nelson Society Journal* of October 2003, when reporting these plans, asked the question *"What are you going to do?"* This is my contribution.

Peter Nelson
July 2005

* Readers may be interested in finding out more about The Nelson Society at www.nelsonsociety.org.uk and its sister organisation, The 1805 Club, at www.admiralnelson.org

The *HMS Victory* website at www.admiralnelson.org is also worth visiting.

Picture Postcard Monthly information, as well as a host of other detail to do with postcard collecting, can be found at www.postcardcollecting.co.uk, which is the website of Reflections of a Bygone Age.

NOTES - Postcards and Nelson

I have tried to avoid using technical postcard terms, as far as I was able, but inevitably one or two are used and need explanation.

Words and Definitions:

Undivided back:	As distinct from divided back cards, such cards were printed before January 1902 and only had space for the address on the non-picture side of the card. It was expected that messages would be written on the picture side.
Real Photographic:	This describes a postcard produced by a photographic rather than a printing process. Such cards are usually glossy in appearance and show greater, clearer detail.
Hand-coloured:	Coloured by hand - usually by one of a team of women paid a small sum of money for every 1,000 cards painted.
Montage:	Combining of several smaller pictures on a card to create a particular effect or tell a story.
Scarce:	Not found easily - a card that collectors tend to hold on to.
Rare:	Few actually exist.
Vignette:	A small picture or addition. More generally used now to describe a borderless picture that occupies only part of the face of the card.
Modern:	Always debated but generally post-1950. Cards usually larger than standard size
Standard Size:	5½ inches x 3½ inches (140 x 89 mm)

An extensive range of Nelson postcards was published, particularly between 1900 and the outbreak of World War One - the *Golden Age* referred to by postcard collectors. Though all the major postcard publishers produced cards (sometimes sets of cards or series) there are still many postcards around today whose publishing history is unknown. Collectors need to be discriminating. There are thousands of postcards of Nelson's Column and of HMS *Victory*, yet relatively very few of other places or objects associated with Nelson's life. Postcard values reflect this. *Victory* is, nevertheless, an interesting collecting theme, particularly when the history of the ship is studied, and some cards of Nelson's Column, such as the 1905 Centenary ones, are scarce.

Postcard condition is also relevant, particularly to value. A collector of Nelson postcards will quickly become aware of the range of quality and variation of condition that affect price as in any other area of collecting.

Postcards sometimes differ in other ways. Publishers frequently produced the same picture in monochrome and in colour, for example. Collectors often find that there are other variations of what, at first, seem to be the same postcards. Commonly, these are variations in caption - a word or several are changed. Sometimes the difference is a pre-printed message on the back of one and not on the other. Such things are found unexpectedly and add interest to collecting!

The majority of postcards illustrating this book should be readily collectable and for every one appearing here there are many more. Most of the selected postcards date from the 1905 centenary period but I have also included some of the many attractive modern postcards available today. I have included particular details of each of the 200 postcards used as illustrations - the title of the card, the publisher if known, the postcard series and the number given to the postcard by the publisher.

I mentioned David Shannon's catalogue in my introduction. David's listing, which covered about 400 known postcards at its date of publication in 1987, was deliberately focused on the key Nelson cards and sought to list only significant *Victory* and Trafalgar Square postcards, for example. *Victory* and Trafalgar Square postcards are very common and one could probably produce a book/list of *Victory* postcards alone! Don't ignore them, though. While, certainly, there is a huge variety, some *Victory* postcards are interestingly different in detail and some are constituent parts of Nelson sets and are, therefore, important for that reason. *Victory* postcards record the pre-restoration state of the ship, the stages of its eventual restoration and the state of the ship today. They show detail of the ship and provide a helpful background against which to appreciate the Nelson story.

You may also like to do what I have done, which is to widen my collecting range. I collect, for example, cards of other ships that have carried Nelson's name. There are, of course, other Nelson-related themes that offer a choice to the collector looking for an original slant. Ships named after Nelson's battles or ships named after those that fought at Trafalgar might be themes that would appeal to collectors with a particular maritime partiality.

If you wish to collect postcards in the United Kingdom, you will want to find a variety of sources of cards. There is a long-established but changing diary of Postcard Fairs advertised through *Picture Postcard Monthly* and *Antique Fair* magazines, and one or two dealers are usually present at most Antique Fairs of any size. Many dealers now have their own web sites and shops and offer, in addition, 'approvals' services (they post you cards which match your stated interest and you buy or return them).

The Postcard Traders Association website at www.postcard.co.uk is a good source of information and gives dealer details. It links to the *Picture Postcard Monthly* website. More recently, Internet auction sites such as www.ebay.com have increased in popularity as they make it possible for postcard collectors to buy from sources all over the world. The number of Nelson postcards being advertised has risen significantly since the beginning of 2005 and there has been a corresponding rise in the price of some cards. There are, though, still many bargains for collectors.

If you become seriously interested in postcard collecting you will almost inevitably wish to know more about the history of postcard collecting, postcard publishers and so on. There are very good books which will help, and more details can be found from, for example, *Picture Postcard Monthly*'s website. Anthony Byatt's *Picture Postcards and their Publishers* is a classic reference work which is, unfortunately, out-of-print at present. Occasionally first edition copies can be found on the Internet but they are becoming quite pricey. If you find a copy in the local second-hand bookshop at a reasonable price, grab it! A book that has been reprinted and which is also a valuable reference, particularly for newcomers to postcard collecting, is AW Coysh's *The Dictionary of Picture Postcards in Britain 1894 - 1939*.

Part One
Nelson: The Story

Chapter One - Nelson's Life and Death

Although thousands, possibly millions, of cards were published on the subject of Nelson, several firms only produced a few designs. Of those publishers who offered an extended coverage of Nelson, including his early life and events in his career, Gale and Polden and a yet to be identified company which published a 'Pictorial Post Card' series stand out. Also significant in this area was the output of Giesen Bros. and Woolstone Bros. (Milton series).

Gale and Polden published from London, Portsmouth and Aldershot, and enjoyed a major share of the military and naval markets. Their *Nelson Series* cards were usually a product of their Portsmouth premises, but examples exist of Nelson cards that bear the 'Wellington Series' or Aldershot logo. Gale and Polden often produced the same picture in monochrome and colour and often reprinted after long gaps. Their numbering system was elaborate - for example *E/No325/G&P/268* - but as all the company records prior to World War 1 were lost in a fire at Aldershot, it is a challenge to track down all the cards produced.

The publishers of the 'Pictorial Post Card' series covered the story of Nelson's life from his birthplace and leaving home to his going to sea and events thereafter. These postcards crop up in most dealers' boxes, so they must have been printed in exceptional quantities. The identity of the publisher has yet to be confirmed which, considering the size of the output and the number of cards in the range, is surprising. Gold-bordered, these cards were produced in two sizes, standard and a smaller 83 x 120mm size. Sometimes they are only printed with the words 'Post Card' on the back, instead of the full title. A strong contender is JJ Coleman, an East Anglian firm, which gave away the cards in its starch boxes. P. Lankester & Co. of Tunbridge Wells also produced postcards with the same wording, 'Pictorial Post Card', on the back of their topical photographic cards produced from 1904. The same firm marketed penny-in-the-slot postcard machines, and it could be that Lankester was the publisher of the 'Nelson' Pictorial Post Cards, though, as some of the cards can be found with undivided backs, that could rule them out. Until the mystery is solved and the publisher's identity established, Pictorial Post Cards must remain listed under 'unidentified publisher'.

Gale and Polden cards and Pictorial Post Cards could be the basis for a collection focusing on major events in Nelson's life, but there are other choices, including the previously mentioned JJ Keliher and Co. Ltd. and Raphael Tuck and Sons, who also published extended ranges.

In making my own choices for inclusion of publishers in this book, I have tried to be representative rather than to reflect comparative publisher output or quality.

The Old Rectory in which Lord Nelson was born, now demolished.

The Horatio Nelson story begins here. Nelson wrote that he was born in this house, the Burnham Thorpe Parsonage in Norfolk, on 29 September 1758. His father, Edmund, was the Rector of Burnham Thorpe and the father of eleven children of whom eight survived. The third boy was Horatio who, in 1767, suffered a hard early blow when his mother Catherine, who was related to the famous Walpole family, died.

Nelson was to return to the Parsonage when 'on the beach' and without a ship for five years after his marriage in 1787. He occupied himself with coursing, gardening and digging out a large pond in the grounds, but his wife never came to terms with the cold, draughty building.

The Parsonage House, as Nelson called it, was demolished in 1802, three years before his death, by the Reverend Everard, so postcard illustrations and other representations rely heavily on a painting of it by Francis Pocock that is now is in the National Maritime Museum at Greenwich.

This card, posted in 1905, promises *"I have sent you the birthplace of Lord Nelson 1½ miles distance from Creake."* Unfortunately not so! Nevertheless it is an interesting card to add to a Nelson collection.

This Rectory, one hundred metres west of the site of the original, was built at the beginning of the nineteenth century. A wall separates the grounds from the village road running past. A signpost points to the area of Nelson's birthplace and a plaque on the wall beside the path tells the visitor that the original rectory stood twenty yards back from the wall. The southern end of the grounds still show the evidence of the large ship-sized pond dug by Nelson, with the help of the gardener, when he was trying to occupy himself while 'on the beach'.

Bob Brister, in his booklet *A Journey Around Nelson's Norfolk*, reported local gossip that 'there are suggestions' that Nelson might have been born in a nearby farmhouse rather than in the parsonage. Tom Pocock, writing in *The Nelson Companion*, gives a little more detail regarding 'persistent traditions' in the village (Burnham Thorpe) that place his birth at either a former farm known as *The Shooting Box* (the family lived there during redecoration of the Parsonage) or at *Ivy Farm* where his mother was taken from church experiencing premature labour. Another contender was a barn that was an outbuilding of the local hostelry, *The Plough* (which features later in the book).

This rather faded postcard seems to be of a farmhouse. The *www.norfolkcoast.co.uk* website features a 1937 photograph of the same building which is captioned as '*said to be part of Burnham Thorpe Rectory*'. That building is known to have been demolished in 1802, unlike this one, which clearly was strongly associated with Nelson for some reason. Could this be the Shooting Box or Ivy Farm? Or is it some other contender for the site of the great man's birth?

All Saints Church, Burnham Thorpe, where Nelson's father was Rector from 1775 to 1802. He is now buried in the chancel. Horatio Nelson was baptised here and had expected to be buried here, too, but the nation had other plans for a national hero and laid him to rest in St Paul's Cathedral.

The church was struck by lightning in the 1790s and later repaired in 1820. It fell into disrepair again later in that century. It was restored again, following an appeal by the Prince of Wales (later Edward V11) and the Admiralty, as part of the 1905 Trafalgar Centenary preparations. The Navy Ensign that is sometimes flown from the church tower is a replica incorporating the early Union Flag, which, before 1801, had no red cross of St. Patrick as a part of it.

The church now has strong naval associations with ensigns from HMS *Indomitable,* which were flown at the Battle of Jutland, a cross, lectern and other pieces made from the timbers of HMS *Victory* and a bronze crest and ensigns from HMS *Nelson,* the last battleship to bear the Nelson name. This was presented to the church in 1955 on the 150th anniversary of the Battle of Trafalgar. There are also documents and items associated with Nelson to be seen at the church.

Both of Nelson's parents are buried inside the church, while his brother Maurice and sister Susannah are buried in the churchyard.

6. *Burnham Thorpe Church. The Font Where Nelson was Christened - publisher unknown, no. 94529*

The font is made from Purbeck marble, the bowl being decorated in 13th century style. The base and support are of a later period. It is still used today.

It is presumed that, as he had been born prematurely and was weak, Nelson was privately baptised at this font on 9 October. He was later publicly baptised on 15 November 1758.

There are differing accounts explaining a confusion regarding his name. For many years, through boyhood, at least until aged eleven, he preferred to use the name Horace. He began to be known as Horatio at about the time he joined his first ship, though his father, who by many accounts preferred the name *H*oratio, as an old man still referred to his son in letters as Horace.

This lectern, the rood beam and the cross above it were made from the timbers of the *Victory*.

The rood beam was a gift from the women of Canada in Nelson's memory. The lectern was carved from wood given by the Admiralty in 1887. Copper plates at the base carry information for visitors.

Lectern, made of wood from the old "Victory," given by the Lords of the Admiralty.

Below is actually a picture of the public house in Burnham Thorpe, *The Lord Nelson*, which was built in 1650. Nelson knew it as *The Plough*, by which name it was known until 1807 when it was re-named in his honour. There is another version of this postcard with the same number and identical except for the title which is '*Nelsons Inn, Burnham Thorpe. Where Nelson gave a farewell dinner before his last voyage*'.

Nelson was very familiar with the inn and held a party there for his relatives and friends just before he left to take command of the *Agamemnon* in February 1793, taking with him many local men.

During the tenancy of Mr Les Winter, which began in 1966, it became a sort of living museum, housing memorabilia, paintings, etc and serving *Nelson's Blood*, a special blend that included rum. The name *Nelson's Blood* has long been a nickname for rum in the Navy, originating from a spurious tale that Nelson's body had been preserved in a cask of rum (actually brandy and spirits of wine) that had then been issued to the crew of the *Victory*.

David and Penny Thorley have *The Lord Nelson* now and they have, as can be seen by visiting the pub or the web site (*www.nelsonslocal.co.uk*), maintained the traditions and character. The pub remains much the same as it always has been. There is no bar and all drinks are dispensed from the taproom. Beer is served straight from the barrel for the customers who still enjoy the age-old settles with which Nelson would probably be familiar were he able to call in today - and *Nelson's Blood* is still supplied too!

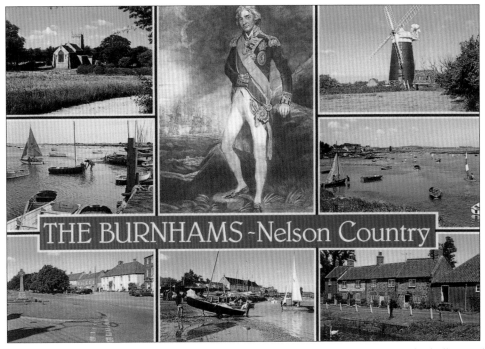

This is obviously a 'modern' card but many older postcards of the Burnhams, including real photographic examples, can be found which give a good idea of the countryside in which Nelson grew up. The original seven 'Burnhams' were Burnham Westgate, Burnham Ulph, Burnham Sutton, Burnham Norton, Burnham Overy, Burnham St Edmunds and Burnham St Andrews. Burnham Thorpe replaced the last two of these.

Burnham Market replaced the first three and Burnham Overy Staithe developed to replace Burnham Overy Town as the chief outlet to the sea. Burnham Overy (the 'sea' pictures above), one of seven original 'Burnhams' in the area, is a small village on the north Norfolk coast not far from Burnham Thorpe. It is probable that this is where Nelson first saw the North Sea, then called the German Ocean. This was a busy seaport in Nelson's day, now silted up, and he visited often when young and when unemployed. He rode or walked along the tidal creek here following the Overy embankment to a favourite, quiet spot to read the latest news when the *Norfolk Chronicle* arrived with the mail coach each Saturday.

Norwich Grammar School.
(of which Nelson was a Scholar.)

"Nelson's Statue" near by.

Nelson attended three schools before extending his practical education by going to sea. He went as a boarder to the first, the Royal Grammar School in the Cathedral Close at Norwich, when he was about nine years of age. The statue seen on this postcard was erected in 1847 and stands outside the Grammar School. After attending his next school in Downham Market he went to his third school, the more modern Paston School at North Walsham. Here he was taught French and certainly became familiar with the works of Shakespeare from which he quoted readily in later life. Paston School has a small Nelson Museum and boasts a classroom where Nelson was educated, and also a brick bearing the HN initials and a pencil box he must have forgotten to take with him when he left.

At the age of twelve, Nelson asked to go to sea with his uncle, Captain Maurice Suckling, who was something of a hero. In 1759 on the 21 October, a date that was to prove significant again at the end of Nelson's life, his uncle had successfully defeated the French in the Caribbean. He had been called back from the 'beach' in 1770 to captain *Raisonnable* and agreed to find a place for his nephew.

This postcard shows the young (and rather small for a twelve-year old) Nelson about to leave home. Though the man in the picture is probably meant to represent his widower father, the identity of the lady is unclear. Nelson made the six-hour journey to Chatham on his own, found his way to the ship, and there began his naval service as a midshipman.

Nelson leaves home to go to Sea
for the first time. 1771.

NELSON'S FIRST FAREWELL. *(From the Picture by George W Joy.)*

This postcard is probably another flight of fancy, but at least Nelson looks his age! Nelson's mother and maternal grandmother, who had lived with the family, had died within five days of each other in 1767, so the identity of the lady in the picture is anyone's guess.

12. *Nelson's First Farewell (from the picture by George W Joy) - published by Cassell and Co. Ltd. Cassell's Saturday Journal Postcard*

Nelson at twelve years of age waiting to embark
on board the "Raisonnable" of sixty-four guns. A.D. 1771.

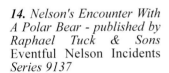

13. Nelson at twelve years of age waiting to embark on board the Raisonnable *of sixty-four guns. AD 1771 - publisher unknown (Pictorial Post Card)*

Nelson joined the *Raisonnable* at Chatham and experienced his first taste of life on board a warship. Preparing to go to sea as a result of the Falklands dispute, the ship was refitting and eventually left to go to Sheerness. At the last minute a settlement of the dispute made her future uncertain, so uncle and nephew parted company; Captain Suckling to *Triumph* and his nephew to join a West Indiaman and to go to the Caribbean.

Nelson, now in the merchant navy, gained much practical experience from his year's secondment, and benefited from seeing an alternative regime for managing men. This was to shape his attitude to command later.

Re-united with his uncle in 1772, Nelson had obviously learned enough to be given command of one of *Triumph*'s boats and now learned to navigate the Thames. He saw two ships, *Carcass* and *Racehorse,* being prepared for a voyage towards the North Pole and was captivated by the plan to explore the unknown. He asked to join the expedition and his uncle agreed to him joining one of the two ships, the *Carcass*, as coxswain.

14. Nelson's Encounter With A Polar Bear - published by Raphael Tuck & Sons Eventful Nelson Incidents Series 9137

This was a scientific expedition in the spirit of the Cook expedition to the Southern ocean and, when it set sail in June 1773, Nelson was to make his mark. In charge of a cutter, he helped save some of the *Racehorse* men from angry walruses. Later, wanting a bear skin for his father, he set off with a companion to try to shoot a bear. The fourteen-year old was saved by the ice opening up and a cannon fired from his ship. His musket had failed but he had still planned to hit the bear with the butt end. Though foolish, he impressed his captain with his bravery. The expedition learned little that was new, but no doubt Nelson did.

15. Nelson Volunteering To Board A Privateer In A Gale - published by E. Wrench Ltd. no. 10499

On his return, Nelson joined the frigate *Seahorse* and left for the East Indies, where he stayed for about two and a half years. He was sent home on the *Dolphin* after succumbing to a serious paralysing fever and survived the voyage home, during which he claimed to have experienced a vision of light which prompted his decision to risk everything in the future for his country.

He had recovered on arrival, and thanks to his uncle who was now Comptroller of the Navy, he was fit to be appointed to *Worcester* sailing to Gibraltar.

On his return from the 'Rock' he passed his promotion examination and was appointed as second Lieutenant to the *Lowestoffe* captained by William Locker, which was destined for the West Indies. In later years he corresponded regularly with William Locker, who in 1793 was appointed lieutenant governor of Greenwich Hospital.

While in the West Indies, Nelson was involved in a number of adventures including the one pictured here. He was also given his first independent command, a schooner *Little Lucy*, which was a captured prize.

From this point his career took off and he was appointed Captain of *Hinchinbroke* in 1779, the first step on the ladder leading to flag rank. He was kept busy as Britain was fighting the Americans, French and, from 1779, Spain.

10499   NELSON VOLUNTEERING TO BOARD A PRIVATEER IN A GALE.

16. Ruins of marriage place of Lord Nelson, Nevis, W.I. - published by A. Moure Losada, no. 105a

Nelson returned to the West Indies in command of the frigate *Boreas*, arriving in Antigua at the end of July 1784. He was a vastly more experienced sailor, having been to the Baltic in command of *Albermarle* and across the Atlantic to North America, where he his crew suffered from scurvy - something he was careful to avoid in the future. He had also been to the West Indies with Lord Hood's fleet.

This time he fell in love with Frances Nisbet, the widowed daughter of the senior judge of Nevis. Nelson was keen to marry Frances, who was attractive, well-to-do and was a good 'catch'. After eighteen months, Nelson married her on 11 March 1787 under a silk cotton tree at Montpelier Plantation, the home of her uncle the President, on the island of Nevis - a marriage destined to end in ruins, like the house of which only the gateposts remain today.

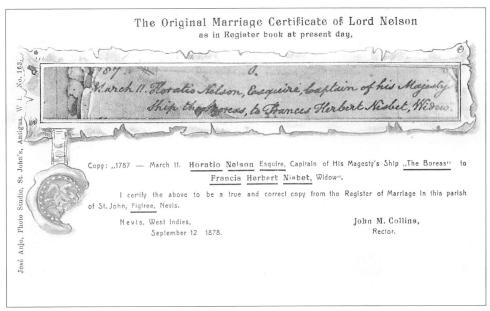

This postcard shows a copy of the entry in the St John's Church Register of the details of the marriage of Horatio Nelson and Frances Herbert Nisbet. A postcard later in the book shows the interior of the church at Figtree.

Nelson's marriage coincided with his recall to England. His wife followed a few months later. Frances had a six-year old son, Josiah, by her previous marriage. He was eventually taken to sea by his step-father in 1793.

Back in England, Frances and Horatio travelled around for a while visiting friends and dealing with Admiralty business. They went to Bath and the West Country, finally settling in Burnham Thorpe in 1788. The marriage was strained immediately. Nelson was stressed by not being employed and his wife was unsettled by having to live in a cold and draughty house in one of the coldest parts of England. He wanted work and children: she wanted warmth - and no family came along.

*18. Nelson Loses His Right
Eye - published by Raphael
Tuck & Sons Eventful Nelson Incidents Series 9137*

England was now at peace and Nelson had to suffer five years of frustrating inactivity (as far as sea service was concerned) on half pay of eight shillings a day, living back at home in Burnham Thorpe. He constantly pestered the Admiralty for appointment to a ship, but also tried his hand at farming in a small way. Frances found Norfolk to be unbearably cold, while Nelson grew increasingly disturbed by the news of the French Revolution that began in 1789 and threatened the stability of England.

Finally recalled to the sea, Nelson and Josiah Nesbit sailed in *Agamemnon* under Lord Hood to the Mediterranean where, following a successful blockade of Toulon, the city fell to the French Royalists. Nelson was sent to Naples to try to persuade the King of Naples and the Two Sicilies to support with reinforcements. Here he met the British Envoy, Sir William Hamilton, and his wife Emma.

Nelson then fought his first major sea battle, taking on several French ships and almost sinking one frigate.

Toulon was re-taken by the Revolutionary army led by a young officer called Bonaparte, and the British had to find a new naval base in the area. An attempt was made to take Corsica and, during an attack on Calvi on 12 July 1794 using guns landed from his ship, Nelson was injured when an exploding shell blew stones into his right eye. He lost the sight of that eye but bravely carried on.

19. The Battle of St Vincent, 14 February 1797 - published by Raphael Tuck & Sons Nelson Centenary *Series 6692*

THE BATTLE OF ST VINCENT, FEBRUARY 14TH 1797.

Nelson's first fleet action followed in March 1795 in which he engaged the *Ca Ira* - an 80-gun French ship - and reduced it to a floating wreck. Other action followed and with it, his appointment as Commodore.

In 1796 he took command of the 74-gun *Captain* when *Agamemnon* needed an overhaul and, later, the *Minerve* for a while acting independently of the fleet. Back in *Captain* by February 1797, he was in time to take part in the Battle of Cape St Vincent in which the British fleet was heavily outnumbered by the Spanish Grand Fleet.

Breaking with all precedent because he saw the danger of the Spanish fleet escaping, Nelson, against the orders of Admiral Jervis and the tradition of maintaining line of battle, broke out of that line and placed his ship where it would block the escape of the enemy. In doing so, he risked not only his ship, faced with overwhelming odds, but also his career and his life.

Though his ship was heavily punished, eventually dismasted and badly damaged, Nelson, now supported by other ships, put her alongside the 80-gun *San Nicolas*, herself entangled with the 112-gun *San Josef*. Nelson led the boarding party that captured *San Nicolas* before using her as a bridge to board the *San Josef*. The enemy had also suffered terrible damage caused by the superior gun-handling of the English ships, and the Spanish officers - their Admiral fatally wounded - offered Nelson their swords.

Nelson's tactical awareness and bravery had been witnessed by the fleet and his fame was assured.

20. The Wounded Spanish Commodore surrendering the San Nicolas *to Nelson - published by Gale & Polden Ltd. The* Nelson *Series*

The Wounded Spanish Commodore surrendering the "San Nicolas" to Nelson.

21. Battle of St Vincent AD 1757. Nelson embraced by his superior Officer Admiral Jervis in gratitude & admiration after the Battle - publisher unknown (Pictorial Post Card)

Battle of S.t Vincent A.D.1797.
Nelson embraced by his superior Officer
Admiral Jervis in gratitude & admiration after the Battle.

Nelson had set a precedent by acting on his own initiative but his gamble had paid off. In other circumstances he would, in all likelihood, have paid with his career. Not in this case!

The battle won, Nelson was thanked and congratulated by a grateful Jervis. The scene is captured on this postcard, one of many which show the separate individual battles and heroic acts of the man.

Nelson's reward was popular fame and to be created a Knight of the Bath. With his latest honour came the news of his promotion to Rear-Admiral.

Following the battle of Cape St Vincent, Nelson, with Miller his Flag Captain, moved to the strife-torn 74-gun *Theseus* and a crew on the verge of mutiny.

Two weeks later, the *Theseus* was a changed ship and, with a loyal crew, she took part in the Cadiz blockade.

In early July 1797, in the course of the blockade, Nelson, in the ship's launch, joined in an effort to save a bomb ketch, the *Thunderer*, that was attacked by a number of small Spanish craft. While engaged in fierce hand-to-hand fighting. Nelson's life was twice saved by his coxswain, John Sykes, who was seriously hurt as a consequence.

Once again Nelson was victorious - and the legend was beginning to grow.

22. Nelson attacks a Spanish Launch July 3rd 1797 - publisher unknown (Pictorial Post Card)

Nelson loses his arm in the night attack on the Mole at Santa Cruz. A.D. 1797.

Probably because of the strategic flair that he had demonstrated in February and his recent bravery at Cadiz, Nelson was ordered to lead an attempt to capture the Spanish-held Tenerife port of Santa Cruz on 24 July 1797.

Difficulties with weather and tides upset the plan, and the essential element of surprise was lost. The landings of marines and crewmen had to be aborted and a frontal attack employed instead. Nelson, of course, led from the front and, as he drew his sword on landing, he was severely wounded by grapeshot.

His life was probably saved this time by his stepson, Josiah Nisbet, who found him, got him into a boat, and with help got him back to a ship. With a tourniquet on his arm, he was then rowed back to his flagship, *Theseus,* which he climbed aboard unaided. There the surgeon removed his right arm. Nelson acknowledged that Josiah had saved his life and that he should have died within ten minutes without his aid.

Nelson presented with the Freedom of the City of London & Gold Casket of 100 guineas value. Chamberlain's Office, Guildhall, Nov. 1797.

Invalided home aboard the frigate *Seahorse,* Nelson arrived back in England on 1 September 1797. He met his family in Bath and eventually travelled to London, where he was presented with the freedom of London at Guildhall on 28 December 1797 by the Chamberlain, John Wilkes. His wound caused him great pain until the ligature came away when the stump of his right arm was able to heal.

Norwich, the nearest major city to his place of birth, also honoured him with a grant of Freedom of the City and a substantial sum of money.

24. *Nelson presented with the Freedom of the City of London & Gold Casket of 100 guineas value. Chamberlain's Office. Guildhall, Nov. 1797 - publisher unknown (Pictorial Post Card)*

25. Part of the first letter written by Nelson after the loss of his right arm - publisher unknown (Pictorial Post Card)

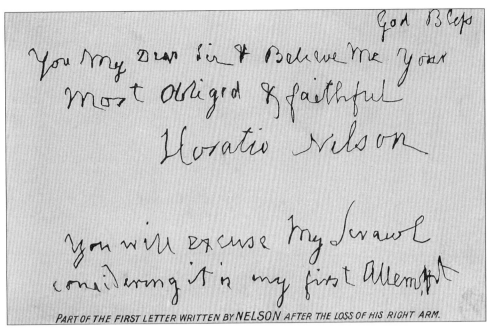

25. Part of the first letter written by Nelson after the loss of his right arm - publisher unknown (Pictorial Post Card)

PART OF THE FIRST LETTER WRITTEN BY NELSON AFTER THE LOSS OF HIS RIGHT ARM.

Nelson was a prolific letter-writer all his life and, of course, had to learn to write with his left hand after his injury at Santa Cruz.

Though he could have employed a secretary, he preferred to write his own letters to which he added different signatures as his titles changed.

26. Battle Of The Nile, August 1st , 1798 - publisher JJ Keliher & Co. Ltd

BATTLE OF THE NILE, August 1st, 1798.

In December 1797, Nelson was promoted Rear Admiral of the Blue and appointed to the 74-gun *Vanguard,* which was to join Admiral St Vincent in the Mediterranean. In April 1798, he joined the fleet and was given command of a squadron of eight ships watching a numerically superior French fleet in Toulon, which intelligence had told him was there to guard a French army of 40,000. Due to Nelson's temporary absence, caused by storm damage done to his ships, the French fleet sailed for an unknown destination.

Nelson, now reinforced by more ships but short of scouting frigates, guessed that Egypt was the destination. He set sail and, unknowingly, reached Alexandria before the French.

He searched the coast and, when he returned, discovered the French army had been landed but that the French fleet was still moored in Aboukir Bay. When Nelson arrived in late afternoon of 1 August 1798, the French fleet of thirteen, including the 120-gun *L'Orient,* flagship of Admiral Brueys, was anchored close to the shore in shoal water where the Admiral believed it to be relatively safe.

N 3 ROTARY PHOTO. E.C.   BATTLE OF THE NILE, NELSON

Not expecting an attack late in the day, the French only cleared their seaward guns for action when they realised Nelson was not going to delay.

Putting into action Nelson's prepared plan, some of his captains - his 'band of brothers' as he called them - took their ships between the anchored enemy and the shore, while the rest attacked from seaward. In the course of the action, Nelson was wounded in the head but was back in action in time to see *L'Orient* blow up and the victory complete.

It was an overwhelming victory, and all Nelson's ships were still afloat. Only four French ships escaped burning or capture, and French casualties totalled 5,000. Nelson had lost 200 men, while 700 were injured.

This modern postcard shows one of the many pictures painted of the battle and in particular the moment just before *L'Orient* disintegrated. The picture was painted by George Arnald (1763 - 1841).

Modern research has shown that her main powder magazine exploded, blowing off her stern, an event shortly followed by the detonation of her forward magazine at 10pm. The cumulative explosion was catastrophic, leading to the deaths of hundreds of French sailors, many of whom drowned as the ship sank within minutes. The noise was so overwhelming and stunning that the battle halted for a while.

29. Lord Nelson wounded at the Nile, August 1st, 1798 - published by JJ Keliher & Co Ltd

The scale of Nelson's victory at Aboukir was so great that, in modern vernacular, he shot to stardom.

Taking months to reach home, the news arrived in England on 2 October, travelled across Europe and eventually the world. With it spread Nelson's fame. The victory ended Napoleon's Eastern ambitions and the specific threats to Turkey and India. His army was left isolated in Egypt and, in maritime terms, the French had lost any control of their coastal waters in the Mediterranean and could no longer move with any safety.

Nelson, though, was also paying a price. He was far from well. After taking time to make his damaged ships seaworthy, he headed for Naples, suffering illness on the way. He was plagued with headaches and vision problems for a while afterwards and possibly suffered, unknowingly, from concussion as a result of his 'Nile' head injury.

30. Horatio, Viscount Nelson, KB Vice-Admiral of the Fleet - published by the National Maritime Museum (copyright NMM)

The largest share of the prize money, paid by the Admiralty for the French ships captured and ordered to be sunk, went to the absent commander-in-chief, Earl St Vincent. He received over £8,000 (equivalent to £400,000 today). Nelson's share as one of six flag captains was about £1,400 (equivalent to £70,000), less than a captain's share of £2,200 (equivalent to £110,000).

Nelson was compensated to some degree by being showered with gifts, money and new titles. Granted a pension of £2,000, he was created a Baron, becoming known as Baron Nelson of the Nile and Burnham Thorpe. The East India Company gave him £10,000, and other countries honoured him with decorations and presents. The Sultan of Turkey, Selim III, sent Nelson a number of gifts, including a musket inlaid with gold and diamonds, but the gift of which Nelson was most proud was the Chelengk or 'plume of Triumph'. Nelson was the first non-Islamite to receive this award, made of thirteen rays of diamonds with a large diamond in the centre, which could be spun by a clockwork mechanism. Nelson wore this amazing piece in his hat.

This portrait of him later in life shows him typically wearing many of his decorations and his Chelengk. Some ridiculed him, accusing him of ostentation, but there is ample evidence that he sought fame, and actively worked for it. This was but one means to that end.

Nelson usually wore two medals round his neck - the King's Naval Gold Medals for the St Vincent and Nile battles, while on his coat he wore the Order of the Bath, the Order of St Ferdinand and Merit, the Turkish Order of the Crescent and the Order of St Joachim (all orders of knighthood). Facsimiles served for everyday wear on board ship and, though tarnished, gave him a unique identity.

31. Arms of Lord Nelson - published by C W Faulkner & Co. Ltd

When Nelson was created a Knight of the Bath, he was permitted to re-define the family coat of arms. He took the opportunity to highlight his achievements by including in the modified design elements to reflect his successes. Some were his ideas - others were suggested by the College of Arms.

As his achievements mounted, so his coat of arms changed to accommodate this. Some of the changes were directly pictorial, such as the seascape in the centre, the sailor holding the commodore's flag (Nelson's idea) and the stern view of the *San Josef* at the top right. Others were emblematic, such as the lion chewing the Spanish and French flags.

The version shown here includes additions reflecting the Nile battle, such as the Chelengk at the top left and the central seascape.

The family motto '*Faith and Works*' was changed to '*Palmam Qui Meruit Ferat*' translated as '*Let him who deserved it bear the palm*'. Both sailor and lion bear the palm in the coat of arms.

Political cartoons, such as the ones by James Gillray, made powerful political and personal comment. In this example, *The Hero of the Nile*, shown on a modern National Maritime Museum postcard, Gillray was taking a swipe at Nelson's vanity. He was pictured as a ridiculously strange, worn-out figure adorned with samples of his gifts from the Sultan of Turkey. Gillray particularly mocked Nelson's habit of wearing the Chelengk in his hat.

The poking of fun extended to Gillray's version of Nelson's coat of arms. Compare this clever satirical Gillray version with the postcard above. Gillray shows a loaded stocking purse or 'miser' containing £2,000 per annum (Nelson's pension as a baron).

Gillray used his caricatures freely against Nelson who, it must be said, offered plenty of good material, particularly in the matter of his later relationship with Emma Hamilton. Another of his cartoons, *JOHN BULL Taking a lunch*, which appeared in at least two forms, appears on a postcard published by the Monmouth Museum and his *The Death of Admiral Lord Nelson* appeared on a postcard pictured later in this section.

32. The Hero of the Nile by James Gillray (1757 - 1815) - published by the National Maritime Museum (copyright NMM)

33. Nelson's Reception At Naples After The Battle of The Nile, August 1798 - published by Raphael Tuck & Sons, Nelson's Famous Victories *Series no. 6692*

Nelson arrived in Naples as a hero. His home on arrival, the Palazzo Sessa, was that of the British Ambassador, Sir William Hamilton and his wife, Emma. Emma, much younger than her husband, made an enormous fuss of Nelson and a great impression on eighteen-year old Josiah Nisbet who fell in love with her. However, it was Nelson enjoying the hero-worship who began a passionate affair with Emma, which would last for the rest of his life.

It marked the end of his amicable relationship with Josiah, whose career was harmed by heavy drinking fuelled by jealousy and resentment. He publicly rebuked Nelson for being unfaithful. Nelson, nevertheless, got Josiah a Captaincy two years later, for which he proved unfit. After 1802, Josiah left the sea on half pay.

Nelson, in the flush of his affair with Emma, did not forget his national duty entirely, and organised the evacuation of the Neapolitan Royal Family to Sicily in late December 1798 when the country was threatened by the advance of the French. The Hamiltons left with him, and the threesome set up house together in Palermo. While remaining in command of his fleet, Nelson was now, for most of the time, ashore. The Neapolitan royal family saw Nelson as their means of reclaiming what they had possessed, and any hope Nelson may have had of a quick return to England was dashed.

34. Lady Emma Hamilton as Ariadne, by George Romney - published by the National Maritime Museum (copyright NMM)

Emma Hamilton, daughter of a blacksmith, was born Amy Lyon, but later was known as Emma Hart. Before her marriage to Sir William Hamilton, she had been the mistress of a number of different men before becoming the mistress of his nephew, Charles Greville MP, with whom she spent four years.

When Greville wished to marry in 1784, he sent Emma to Naples to stay with his uncle, a widower, and probably by plan she became in time the latter's mistress. Marriage followed in 1791 and she became a good wife to the much older Ambassador, gaining the friendship of Queen Maria Carolina of Naples.

Sir William taught her to pose in imitation of classical figures on the vases he loved to collect and she enjoyed performing these 'Attitudes', as they were known, for friends and guests.

Emma was acknowledged to be very attractive, and Nelson fell under her spell. The relationship grew from one of closer and closer friendship to that of lovers by early 1800. Her husband probably knew what was happening but possibly feared losing both her and the strong friendship he had developed with Nelson himself.

The affair became public knowledge and also of increasing concern to Nelson's family, friends and the Admiralty who saw that his mind was no longer fully on his duty and suspected his marriage vows might be being forgotten. His friends tried to warn him but he took offence rather than notice.

A change of the Mediterranean command in June 1799, when an ailing Lord St Vincent returned home and left Lord Keith in overall charge, tested Nelson's divided loyalties.

News of Cardinal Ruffo's success in attempting to reclaim Naples from French-supported rebels encouraged Nelson to sail in support, taking with him the Hamiltons. On arrival he learned that Ruffo had defied the order of the King of Naples that only unconditional surrender was acceptable and had agreed free passage for the rebels.

Despite the agreement, Nelson had many of the rebels arrested. The King later ordered many to be tried and about a hundred men and women were publicly executed.

35. 'Emma' by Johann Heinrich Schmidt (1749-1828) - published by National Maritime Museum (copyright NMM). Nelson kept a copy of this picture with him in the cabin of HMS Victory

36. Model of HMS Foudroyant, *Royal United Service Museum - published by Gale & Polden Ltd*

The trial of the rebel leader, Commodore Prince Francesco Caracciolo, was held in the wardroom of *Foudroyant*, Nelson's new flagship, a model of which is shown on this postcard. The verdict was a death sentence and hanging from the yardarm of Nelson's former flagship, *Minerva*.

Weeks spent in *Foudroyant* in Naples harbour, and later on a cruise to Malta, with Sir William going early to bed, resulted in Nelson and Emma becoming lovers. Their daughter, Horatia, was probably conceived aboard the ship in April or May 1800. Earlier, in February, *Foudroyant* had captured *Généreux*, one of the two French escapees from the Nile battle. A coffin was proudly displayed in the great cabin. Made from wood from the *L'Orient*, the coffin had been a gift from Ben Hallowell, a Nile Captain. Nelson, who was very proud of it, was eventually buried in it. *Foudroyant* witnessed significant events in Nelson's life before its sad demise in 1897, captured on postcards and related later in the book.

Nelson, with continuing health problems, had hoped to return to England in *Foudroyant* and had requested as much when he knew Sir William Hamilton had been recalled. Instead, the threesome - Nelson and the Hamiltons - returned across Europe by coach, taking three to four months on what became a triumphal tour.

11 PORTSMOUTH.-The George Hotel. In which Nelson spent his last Hours in England. - LL

The Nelson travelling party landed at Great Yarmouth on 6 November 1800, where Nelson received a hero's welcome. Yarmouth was a place with which Nelson had strong associations and which today boasts a fine Nelson museum. Hostelries of the time like the *The Star Hotel*, the *Wrestlers* (now *Hardy's*) and the *George* at Portsmouth (destroyed by bombing in World War II) were proud of their Nelson connection. Nelson was to come here, to the *George* on 14 September 1805, take breakfast and leave to board the *Victory* for the last time.

On this occasion, Nelson stayed at the *Wrestlers Inn* and then went to Roundwood, in Suffolk, with the Hamiltons, to the house his wife had bought him, and to which she suggested he should bring his friends. She was not there, and they travelled on to London, meeting his wife, Fanny, at *Nerot's Hotel* (also long gone). Emma was pregnant so the meeting was difficult.

Postcards of hotels, castles and rooms claiming a Nelson association are there to be collected - some more easily than others - but they are not as common as those cards showing scenes of his naval life. A plaque commemorating the association of Nelson with the *George Hotel* can be seen on the outside front wall of the building on this postcard view. The plaque appears in more detail on postcards published by Knight Bros. and others. The LL postcard of the *George Hotel* is easier to find than the next card which shows 'Nelson's Room' in the *Star Hotel*, Yarmouth.

38. Nelson Room Star Hotel, Yarmouth, Proprietor: H. Taylor - published by A Yallop, Great Yarmouth

The Hamiltons went to stay in Grosvenor Square. Nelson was kept busy. He reported to the Admiralty, was presented with an engraved sword at the Guildhall and invited to St James Palace. The King initially spoke to him, then turned away and ignored him. Nelson's decorated appearance and the gossip had done the damage. Later that day Nelson showed his hurt and general unhappiness when he was with his wife at dinner at the Admiralty. Fanny tried to save the marriage, but Nelson's obvious preference for the company of Emma made this a vain hope. Nelson, in turmoil, walked the streets at night and eventually left with the Hamiltons for Fonthill Splendens, William Beckford's house.

Snubbed by traditional society, Nelson found himself entertained during Christmas by some of the fringe elements and was involved in a 'monastic fête'. With his public affair becoming increasingly the subject of wit and sarcastic comment, he returned to London on Boxing Day. A day or two later, his marriage effectively ended with his promotion to Vice Admiral and appointment as second-in-command of the Channel Fleet. Nelson joined his new flagship, which was *San Josef*, one of his captures.

39. The Battle of Copenhagen, April 1801 - published by Raphael Tuck & Sons, Nelson's Famous Victories *Series 6692*

His time in *San Josef* was limited. Early in February, Nelson was appointed as second-in-command to Admiral Sir Hyde Parker's fleet and moved his flag to *St George.* The fleet was to operate in the Baltic to prevent Scandinavia joining a French alliance. News of the birth of his daughter, Horatia, reached Nelson before he joined the fleet and he was able to spend three days with Emma in London before reporting for duty. Even then, the sailing was delayed until 12 March. Denmark, as the most powerful Scandinavian state, was the destination.

40. Nelson's Blind Eye at Copenhagen - published by Raphael Tuck & Sons, Eventful Nelson Incidents *Series 9137*

Nelson was kept short of information by the over-cautious Hyde Parker until it was clear that Denmark would fight rather than surrender its alliance (known as the Armed Neutrality). Nelson apparently offered the hand of friendship to Hyde Parker in the form of a turbot caught en route and, whether this influenced matters or not, his tactical skill was eventually appreciated. He was, nevertheless, unhappy about Parker's cautious approach. Ordered to transfer his flag to *Elephant,* he was allowed to lead the attack on the Danish batteries protecting Copenhagen. Coming under obviously very heavy fire, Parker signalled Nelson to withdraw. Nelson, holding his telescope to his blind eye, ignored Parker's signal, won the battle and then went to see the Prince Royal to negotiate the Peace. Hyde Parker, after initially being acclaimed for the success, was called home and never went to sea again.

Nelson's reward was to be appointed the Commander In Chief and, on 22 May 1801, to be created a Viscount. He was allowed to return home later in June, where he resumed his relationship with Emma.

Fears of a French invasion led to Nelson's recall in July and to a failed attempt to destroy the French invasion fleet in Boulogne. When the threat of invasion receded, Nelson was again allowed ashore in October, at which time he rejoined Emma at the new home she had found for him at Merton Place in Surrey.

Merton cost £9,000 (equivalent to £450,000). Nelson had to borrow a third of the cost from his wealthy agent, Alexander Davison.

41. Nelson's House, Merton - published by Collectors Publishing Series, The Mercury Series

Merton Place was the country idyll of Nelson's dreams. Of moderate size by the standards of the day, it had grounds in which to walk, and its own canal diverted from the River Wandle that was given the nickname 'The Nile'. The Nile was stocked so that Sir William could pursue his hobby of fishing. There were animals, stabling and an artificial mound that allowed for views of the surrounding area.

Emma, who had little financial common sense, spent lavishly and turned Merton Place into a shrine to Nelson and an open glorification of their relationship. Pictures of them and of his battles and even trophies of his victories decorated the house. This grated with visitors and also with Sir William, who, though contributing financially, worried increasingly about his mounting debts. Nelson was equally worried, but could not restrain Emma's spending. Aware of his popularity and trying to forget his money problems, Nelson took his seat in the House of Lords on 29 October 1901 and contemplated giving up the sea for a political career.

No postcards of Merton Place as Nelson knew it exist, the house having been demolished before the estate was sold for re-development in 1846. This postcard is one of several that can be found entitled *Nelson's House Merton* or something similar. None are pictures of his house but are of a different property close by, either named after him, or mistakenly thought to be his actual home. The house on the postcard was actually known as Abbey Gate House or Abbey House and it, too, was demolished in 1904/05. The owners helped Emma Hamilton in 1808 when Merton Place was sold off by Nelson's brother and heir for £12,930 (equivalent to £650,000).

42. The Naval Temple and Round House on the Kymin, Monmouth from an oil painting by JA Evans (1854-1936) - published by Monmouth District Council Museums Service (copyright Nelson Museum, Monmouth)

THE NAVAL TEMPLE and ROUND HOUSE on the KYMIN, MONMOUTH

Many of Nelson's family accepted his relationship with Emma, but his father's religious principles meant he could not renounce his recognition of his daughter-in-law and this had led to tension. Edmund, Nelson's father, had died on 26 April 1802 and Nelson did not attend his father's funeral, offering ill-health as the reason. He was probably influenced in his decision by the thought of an almost certain meeting with his wife.

In July 1802 Nelson set off on holiday with the Hamiltons, going first to Oxford where both he and Sir William received honorary degrees. Nelson's brother William and other members of the family joined the touring party before it proceeded to Wales, where Sir William had estates to visit. En route they called at Blenheim Palace but were snubbed by the Duke of Marlborough, who would not meet them or invite them into his house.

In Monmouth they had a better reception, including a cannon salute from the Naval Temple on the Kymin. Later on their tour the party returned to Monmouth and visited the temple, where they had breakfast in the Pavilion. Nelson was very pleased with the recognition the temple gave to contemporary naval victories and commanders, including himself, and declared that the country needed no other naval monument.

Nelsons Bench Merton Church.

The Church of St Mary the Virgin, where Nelson and his new family worshipped, was within a mile of the house. This postcard shows the restored bench from the box pew used by Nelson and his family that was at the front of the church nearest the altar. The walls of the church nave also display funeral hatchments of Nelson and Sir William Hamilton.

Nelson's popularity led to him being as newsworthy as a celebrity of today. His and Emma's relationship was a scandal which the satirists made the most of. They were the subject of bawdy humour and Sir William was made out to be a sad, impotent figure. The rest of the publishing business regarded Nelson as a live, popular hero, and his obvious personal injuries were regarded by the public as the marks of honour of someone who led by example.

Sir William died on 6 April 1803, just over a month before the fragile peace with France came to an end. That month Nelson spent in lodgings over a saddler's shop in Piccadilly, getting ready for the war he knew would come and in which he would have command in the Mediterranean. When war began again on 14 May 1803, Nelson set off for Portsmouth after attending his daughter's christening in Marylebone. He knew that Emma was pregnant again.

He hoisted his flag in *Victory* on 18 May 1803 but it was only a temporary occupation as he had to meet Admiral Cornwallis who was blockading Brest. *Victory* was needed there and Nelson transferred to the frigate *Amphion,* captained by Thomas Hardy. He patrolled in the Mediterranean before his flagship *Victory* rejoined him in July 1803 at Toulon where he began a long vigil to prevent the French fleet escaping to sea. The French army was preparing to invade England and the situation worsened in December 1804 when Spain, too, declared war on England.

The French finally escaped in January 1805, and Nelson chased their fleet across the Atlantic to the West Indies, just failing to make contact. Guessing that the French had doubled back, he set off for home, arriving to find that Admiral Calder had met the French off Finisterre but had allowed them to reach port.

Nelson had been at sea without leave for over two years when he arrived back at Portsmouth on 18 August 1805. He had gone two years, all but ten days, without setting foot on land. Emma, meanwhile, had given birth to a second daughter in January 1804, who died before being christened. Nelson's health was poor and, although he enjoyed being together again with Emma and Horatia and spending time at home, he knew that he would be called upon before long. He used some of the time to think through his tactics for the fight ahead.

45. HMS Victory *moored off Gosport, showing The Round Tower and Sally Port in the background - publisher unknown*

Destiny waited off Southsea in the shape of the waiting *Victory*.

Nelson was visited at 5am on 2 September by Henry Blackwood of *Euryalus*. He was on his way to report to the Admiralty that Villeneuve had joined forces with the Spanish and was in Cadiz with a large combined fleet.

Nelson followed him to London, knowing that he would probably be needed.

Nelson's dash to the office of the Secretary of State for War and the Colonies in London on 13 September 1805 coincided with a visit to the Minister that morning by Major-General Sir Arthur Wellesley, the Duke of Wellington. The two men met for the only time in Lord Castlereagh's waiting room and for a while, Nelson had no idea to whom he was talking. According to Wellington, Nelson talked only about himself and appeared to be vain and silly.

After Nelson left the room, discovered Wellington's identity and returned, he was, according to Wellington, very different, talking about the role of the navy and his strategy. Wellington was struck by Nelson's charisma. Later he remembered Nelson and his maritime success with gratitude as being fundamental to the post-Trafalgar land victories.

This postcard, a copy of an engraving by JP Knight, records that extraordinary meeting summarised by Wellington who commented, *"I don't know that I ever had a conversation that interested me more"*.

46. 'The Army and Navy' - published by Gale & Polden Ltd

47. Nelson leaving for Trafalgar - publisher unknown (Pictorial Post Card)

Nelson was duly appointed to command and returned to Merton, with Emma, to pack and make his farewells. He seemed to have a premonition of the future and of an unavoidable date with destiny. He arranged a service of Holy Communion during which he exchanged wedding rings with Emma and after packing, having dinner and praying at his daughter's bedside, left at 10.30pm on Friday 13 September.

At Portsmouth, in the *George Hotel*, Nelson met up again with the vicar of Merton whose son was going to sea with him on *Victory*. The vicar was able to take a last note home to Emma.

Word had spread as it seemed to do wherever Nelson went, and a large crowd blocked the streets. Nelson made his way to the beach at Southsea amid the cheers and joined *Victory* on 14 September 1805. She sailed the next day.

He was to take command of Collingwood's fleet but he ordered that no salutes should be fired on his arrival. He did not wish to alert the enemy.

Sir Thomas Masterman Hardy is probably the only other naval officer at Trafalgar who most people could name.

He was, uniquely, the only one of the Trafalgar captains who had been with Nelson in his three other great battles. Nelson marked him out for his bravery when he was 27. He promoted him to Post Captain in

48. Battle of Trafalgar, fought October 21st 1805 - published by J Beagles & Co., no. 606.J

command of his flagship, HMS *Vanguard*, after the Battle of the Nile in 1798, when Hardy was 29 years old.

He went on to captain HMS *Foudroyant, Josef* and *St George*. He became Flag Captain of *Victory* in 1803 and was beside Nelson when the latter was fatally wounded. He took command of the battle, but managed to visit Nelson in the cockpit where he obliged with the famous kiss as Nelson was dying. He was not forgotten after Trafalgar, being created a baronet and being given command of *Triumph*. He was eventually made Rear Admiral in 1825 and he became First Sea Lord in 1830. When he died in 1839, a miniature of Nelson was buried with him in accordance with his wishes. He always remained in touch with Lady Nelson.

49. *Vice-Admiral Lord Collingwood. 1750 - 1810 - publisher JJ Keliher & Co. Ltd, 'Admirals All' Series no. 8*

Cuthbert, Lord Collingwood, was one of Nelson's closest friends. He followed Nelson as First Lieutenant of the *Lowestoffe*, as Captain of *Badger* and then as Captain of *Hinchinbrooke*. Their relationship could have ended when they both fell in love with Mary Moutray, wife of the English Harbour Commissioner in Antigua, but it drew them closer. They sketched each other with mixed success. In 1797 they both fought at Cape St Vincent, where Collingwood showed great bravery and rescued Nelson's ship, *Captain*.

They met up again when Nelson was serving with the Channel Fleet in 1800 but then, in 1805, parted company when Nelson came out to Cadiz where Collingwood was watching the French Fleet. Nelson put Collingwood in charge of one of his planned divisions of the fleet. After Trafalgar, he succeeded Nelson as Commander-in-Chief Mediterranean, dying in 1810. He is buried in the crypt of St Paul's Cathedral, beside Nelson.

Nelson arranging his famous signal before the Battle of Trafalgar Oct 21st 1805.

Nelson arrived off Cadiz on 28 September 1805. Within three days all his captains had dined with him and been told of the plan of attack, the 'Nelson touch', should the French and Spanish fleets come out of port.

They were so well-briefed that when the battle began, further signals were unnecessary. Every captain knew what was expected of him and how that fitted with the overall plan. The French line was to be split and Collingwood had the great responsibility of leading his ships to cut off and destroy the Franco/Spanish rear. Nelson was to break through the centre.

News arrived on 19 October via the eyes of the fleet, the frigates, that the combined enemy fleet under the command of Admiral Villeneuve was emerging from Cadiz harbour. All his ships were at sea by 20 October and Nelson closed on them.

50. *Nelson arranging his famous signal before the Battle of Trafalgar, Oct 21st 1805 - publisher unknown. (Pictorial Post Card)*

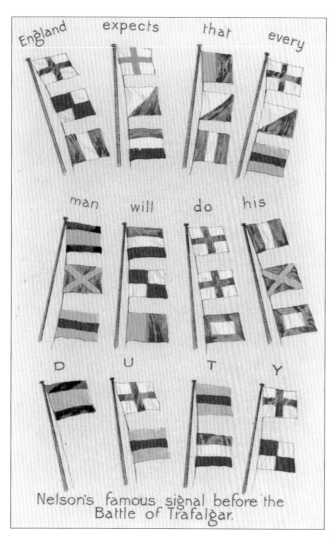

England expects that every
man will do his
D U T Y
Nelson's famous signal before the Battle of Trafalgar.

51. Nelson's famous signal before the Battle of Trafalgar - publisher unknown. (Pictorial Post Card)

As the British fleet sailed towards the enemy fleet on 21 October, Nelson had a special signal hoisted, much to the annoyance of Collingwood who, knowing his orders well, did not welcome what he thought was further direction. Nelson had wanted to send *'England confides that every man will do his duty'* but his flag lieutenant, John Pasco suggested *'expects'* as its inclusion as a substitute reduced the flags needed.

Since then the signal has been frequently misquoted, including the example of the wording of the inscription on Nelson's Column in Trafalgar Square. Collingwood, incidentally, thought the signal wonderful when he saw what it was.

This postcard shows the correct wording of Nelson's signal but the flags shown are not those used at the time. The wrong flag book was used as a reference for many years until the mistake was recognised in 1908 by the Admiralty. As a result, many illustrations, including many postcards produced early in the 20th century, are incorrect. There are variations, too, in the flags arrangements shown particularly pre-1908.

This modern card shows Nelson's signal as it would have been seen at the time. The Popham code provided the 'whole word' arrangements as well as the provision to build words. Nelson's first choice of 'confides' needed spelling out letter by letter whereas 'expects' was a whole word, single flag, no. 269. Surprisingly, the word 'duty' had to be spelled out. The signal was therefore made up of twelve units that would most probably have been hoisted two at a time - a total of six hoists. 'Confides' would have involved additional flag hoists.

52. Lord Nelson's signal at Trafalgar - published by National Maritime Museum no. ENT 32 (copyright NMM)

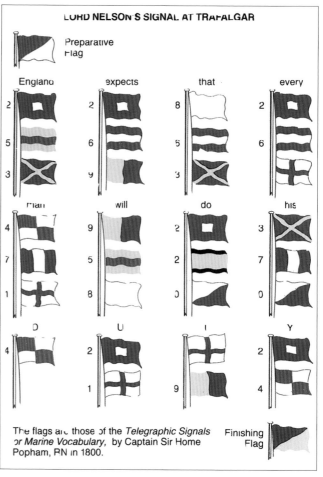

LORD NELSON'S SIGNAL AT TRAFALGAR

Preparative Flag

The flags are those of the *Telegraphic Signals or Marine Vocabulary*, by Captain Sir Home Popham, RN in 1800.

Finishing Flag

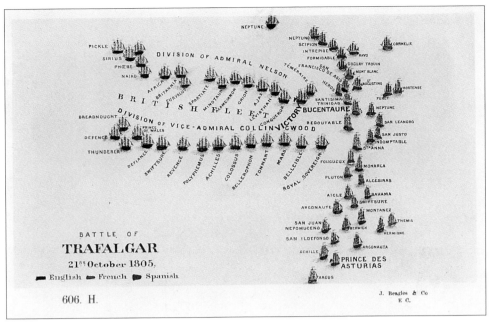

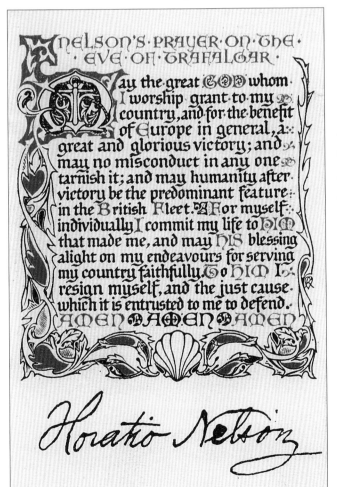

53. Battle of Trafalgar 21 October 1805 - published by J Beagles & Co. no 606.H

Nelson's plan, as explained to his captains before the battle, was one of 'divide and conquer'. His own fleet would split into two divisions, which would cut the Franco/Spanish fleet at pre-selected points. Nelson made clear both the overall strategy and the individual freedom that captains had to take suitable action in the heat of battle. The plan relied on superior seamanship and gunnery, but the crucial difference between the two fleets was that Nelson's captains knew, and had faith in, their leader's strategy. Nelson intended to create confusion, isolate a whole section of the combined enemy fleet, and thereby make concerted opposition less likely.

What is not commonly known is that Villeneuve in his own 'final instructions' to his fleet captains had anticipated Nelson's strategy. What is not understood is why, as the battle developed, there was a failure to defend against Nelson's tactics. Perhaps the French Admiral evaluated the relative fleet strengths and weaknesses, and appreciated that method and means are not always co-incidentally available.

While the fleets were slowly closing, Nelson retired to his cabin and wrote an open letter in which he asked that Emma and Horatia would be looked after should he die. The letter was witnessed by Captain Hardy and Captain Blackwood of *Euryalus*.

Nelson then wrote his now famous prayer. It is read out every Trafalgar Day on the quarterdeck of *Victory*, as well as in many religious services. The original manuscript of the prayer, which is different from this postcard reproduction, uses the word 'who' instead of 'that', and 'light upon' instead of 'alight on'. The word 'it' in the last phrase was not in the original prayer.

The signature reproduced at the bottom of the card is an incongruity. It is typical of Nelson's signature, weeks after losing his right arm in 1797. At the time of Trafalgar he signed himself 'Nelson & Bronte'.

54. Nelson's prayer on the eve of Trafalgar - published by Jarrold & Sons

55. *HMS* Victory *The First Shot at the Battle of Trafalgar - published by J Welch & Sons, Portsmouth*

The First Shot at the Battle of Trafalgar.

The combined enemy fleet of 33 ships of the line outnumbered Nelson's fleet by 6. It also boasted an advantage of 484 guns and, with 30,000 men, a man advantage of 17,000 over the 13,000 at Nelson's command.

Collingwood actually opened the battle by firing a broadside into the Spanish flagship, *Santa Anna,* as he took his ship between her and *Fougeaux.* He sailed across her stern at about 12.20 pm with the rest of his division following.

The Victory breaking the line at the Battle of Trafalgar.

56. *The* Victory *breaking the line at the Battle of Trafalgar - published by J Beagles & Co. no.606.D*

Nelson, meanwhile, was also sailing to break the line and headed for *Santissima Trinidad,* a huge ship with four decks of guns. *Bucentaure,* the following ship, was seen to be carrying the French Admiral, Villeneuve, so Nelson ordered Hardy to change target and sail across her stern.

Victory fired a broadside into *Bucentaure's* stern that did horrific damage as it swept the length of the ship, putting her out of action. As *Victory* passed through the line, she met the *Redoutable* and the two ships began a prolonged fight, during which Nelson was fatally wounded.

Battle of Trafalgar (2.15 p.m.)

The battle, thereafter, became one of ships paired against each other with the enemy van cut off and trying to double back to join the battle. This was to the advantage of the British, who could fire more rapidly and accurately, had confidence in the integrity of their ordnance, and knew their own battle strategy.

Collingwood and his division defeated the rear of the Franco/Spanish column whilst Nelson's division captured the centre.

THE MEN OF THE "REDOUBTABLE" TRYING TO BOARD THE "VICTORY" AT THE BATTLE OF TRAFALGAR.

This postcard shows the *Victory* and *Redoutable* in close proximity during the battle. While this fighting went on, marksmen, who occupied the mast platforms or 'fighting tops' above the hand-to-hand fighting shown here, were firing down at any officer who presented a target.

The isolated van of the enemy tried to intervene but was beaten off. The battle generally developed into many ship-to-ship actions, some of which involved fierce hand-to-hand fighting, during which great heroism was shown. The battle ended at about 4.30pm, with 17 enemy ships captured and another ablaze.

58. *The men of the* Redoubtable *trying to board the* Victory *at the Battle of Trafalgar - published by Cassell & Co. Ltd. Cassell's Art Postcards*

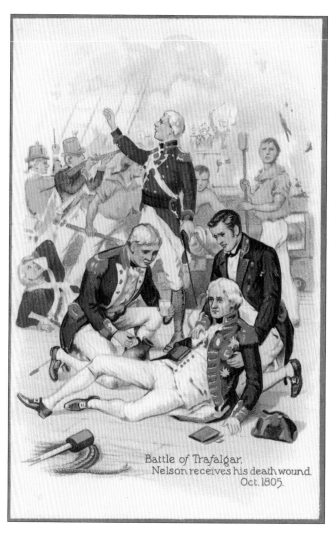

59. Battle of Trafalgar Nelson receives his death wound October 1805 - publisher unknown (Pictorial Post Card)

The joy of the Trafalgar victory was quickly extinguished by grief when the death of Nelson became known throughout the fleet.

Nelson had been shot at about 1.15pm by one of the sharp-shooters in the mizzen-mast fighting tops of the *Redoutable*. He had been advised to cover the imitations of his insignia that he wore on his undress uniform coat, but had declined to change his usual habits. Because of that decision, he was an easily identifiable target on the quarterdeck, even though he would probably have been wreathed in cannon smoke.

Muskets were notoriously inaccurate at that time but the shot, which may or may not have been aimed at him, ultimately proved fatal as the ball passed through his left shoulder epaulette and down into his chest doing irrevocable damage.

60. 'Nelson at the Battle of Trafalgar' by John Schonberg - published by Imperial Fine Art Corporation

Hardy immediately carried Nelson below to the orlop deck, where the surgeon, William Beatty, was able to assess his condition. The bullet had travelled down through his left shoulder, broken two ribs and ripped through his left lung, tearing an artery and going on to break his spine. He was made as comfortable as possible and was able to talk but he was in great pain. At about 3.30pm, Hardy gave him the news that a great victory had been won. Nelson knew, from the moment he was hit, that he was dying and said so. Among his last words were messages for Emma and Horatia.

61. Death of Nelson in the Cockpit of the Victory *Oct 21st 1805 - publisher unknown. (Pictorial Post Card)*

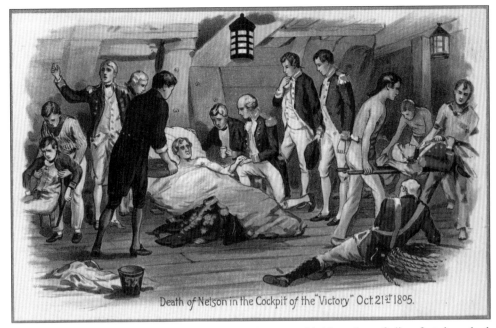

Death of Nelson in the Cockpit of the "Victory" Oct 21st 1805.

Both Beatty and his Chaplain, Alexander Scott, were with him when, fading fast, he asked Hardy to kiss him. Hardy kissed him on the cheek and then his forehead, though Nelson was, by then, delirious and asked who it was. When told he said *"God bless you, Hardy"*. His dying words, at about 4.30pm, followed shortly - *"Thank God I have done my duty"*.

As news of Nelson's death spread through the fleet, hardened sailors broke down in tears. His fellow officers, many of them close friends, were overcome with grief. This was a forerunner of similar scenes across the length and breadth of England when the news reached home.

The news of Nelson's death was carried home by John Lapenotiere in *Pickle*. It took him eight days. He arrived at Falmouth on 4 November and then set off for London by coach, arriving at the Admiralty with his devastating news at 1am on 6 November.

This portrait by Gillray, *The Death of Nelson*, was a comment on the fact that Nelson's death was regarded as the death of a God-like figure.

Was Gillray, who had previously published satirical pictures of Nelson and his relationship with Emma, simply taking a last chance to mock the whole Nelson saga as he had done previously? It would seem so, as Emma Hamilton is posed as Britannia, George III as Captain Hardy and the Duke of Clarence as a sailor. Those who knew Gillray claimed, nevertheless, that he was also motivated by sorrow and pride and the wish to recognise a true hero.

62. The Death of Admiral Lord Nelson from an etching by James Gillray - published by Monmouth District Council Museums Service (copyright Nelson Museum, Monmouth)

63. Britannia Bringing Her Dead Hero To Britannia's Shore - published by Monmouth District Council Museum Service (copyright Nelson Museum, Monmouth)

This postcard of a painting on glass shows Britannia bringing the dead hero home to be immortalised. Britannia associated with Nelson was a theme also used by Sir Benjamin West (1738-1820) who painted *The Immortality of Nelson* in which the dead hero is offered to Britannia by Neptune. Perhaps that is how the word 'immortal' became part of the Nelson story. His 'immortality' was often referred to immediately after his death and a toast to the 'Immortal Memory' has been drunk every Trafalgar night since the tradition began on *Victory*.

Many wished to pass on their memory of Nelson and try to explain what was so special about him. Alexander Scott, the chaplain who attended Nelson as he was dying, wrote of his grief for the loss of "*the most fascinating companion I ever conversed with*" and explained that "*if you live with a man on board a ship for years; if you are continually with him in his cabin, your mind will soon find out how to appreciate him. I could forever tell you the qualities of this beloved man. I have not shed a tear for years before the 21st of October and since, whenever alone, I am quite like a child*".

Such distress was echoed again and again by his friends, acquaintances, seamen and the general public.

Nelson's body, which was expected to arrive by fast frigate, was brought home in *Victory* at the insistence of the crew. *Victory* had needed emergency repair at Gibraltar before making the sad journey home, arriving on 4 December. By this time, arrangements for a funeral had been made.

64. Lord Nelson's Funeral Procession by Water, from Greenwich Hospital to Whitehall, Jan 8th 1806 - published by Monmouth District Council Museum Service (copyright Nelson Museum, Monmouth)

Nelson had anticipated his death and had arranged to have his coffin, made of wood from *L'Orient*, engraved with its history before he left for Trafalgar, telling his agents that he felt he would need it on his return. The coffin was taken out to *Victory* so that his body, which had been preserved in a cask of spirits of wine lashed to the mainmast, could be placed in it. The coffin was then enclosed in lead and later in an outer casket. Nelson's body was then placed on the yacht, *Chatham*, and carried up the Thames to Greenwich to await the official ceremony.

65. *State Barge of King Charles II, which conveyed Nelson's body to Whitehall - publisher unknown (possibly Wright & Logan)*

Charles II's State Barge shown on this postcard can be seen today in the Royal Naval Museum at Portsmouth where it is part of the excellent Nelson exhibition.

The story of the magnificent State funeral for Nelson is one worth reading - the three-day Lying in State in the Painted Hall, the river procession with his coffin carried on this barge, and the huge crowds of silent people. As his body was taken from the water there was an unforgettable moment when the sky grew dark and a squall arrived from nowhere.

The next day, 9 January 1806, the huge procession to St Paul's Cathedral dwarfed the few sailors present, who proudly displayed their battle ensigns to a crowd that acknowledged their victory. The tail of the ticket-only procession had not left Whitehall when the head arrived at St. Paul's Cathedral and the only sound from the crowd was that of hats being removed.

66. *St Paul's Cathedral. Nelson's Tomb - published by Photochrom Co. Ltd*

The Service and Burial in St Paul's Cathedral was both awe-inspiring and a great tribute to a hero. There were 32 admirals and 100 captains in attendance for the five-hour ceremony that concluded in candlelight. Nelson's body was buried in four coffins. The first was the one made from the main mast of *L'Orient* by Ben Hallowell, one of the Nile Captains. This was in turn placed in a coffin of elm, then placed inside another made of lead before being put into the final coffin of elm. The final resting place for the coffins was to be a black marble sarcophagus originally intended for Cardinal Wolsey.

Nelson's family and friends were gathered around and, when the magnificent service came to a conclusion, and the coffin was about to be lowered into the crypt, the sailors present spontaneously tore a large section from the battle flags that were to be placed on the casket. They ripped the section up into smaller mementoes to keep. The significance of this was not lost on some spectators - Nelson belonged to the people and would always belong to the Navy. He was the first commoner to become a nationally popular hero on a scale we are familiar with today.

Part Two
Nelson: What Remains

Chapter Two - HMS *Victory*
- Cathedral and Shrine to Nelson

Postcards of HMS *Victory*, as has already been said in the 'Notes' earlier in the book, are numerous, and many are repetitive views. There are, though, other postcards that show the ship in detail, different periods in her life, how she has changed in the course of restoration and how she looked on special occasions. With the advent of flash photography, it was possible for below-deck views to be presented more readily, including the cockpit area where Nelson died - so many of the internal areas of the ship have also appeared on postcards.

Some postcard publishers, particularly Wright & Logan and Gale & Polden, produced the largest range of HMS *Victory* cards, though Photochrom, Misch and others also published postcards of HMS *Victory* showing detail of decks, rigging etc. These were often sold in sets of six in printed-paper packets. Sets of Wright & Logan postcards, for example, are relatively easy to find and if found with the original packet so much the better. Judging by the frequency with which they turn up in dealers' boxes, they were probably bought by most visitors to the ship and went into reprints. The quality of the Wright & Logan cards, particularly, has ensured their survival in large numbers. Many more recently published cards can be found with a 'posted on board Victory' stamp on their back, too.

In this section, I have aimed to show a selection of views of *Victory*, whole or part, as well as give an idea of the variety of types of postcard that are there to be collected. Other postcards of *Victory* and information about associated Trafalgar Day traditions and *Victory*'s symbolic importance appear elsewhere in the book. HMS *Victory* postcards form a very large sub-category of Nelson-related postcards and one that I am certain collectors will find rewarding.

67. HMS Victory *and Portsmouth Harbour - published by Gale & Polden Ltd*

H.M.S. Victory and Portsmouth Harbour.

Some of the best *Victory* postcards are those that show her as thousands saw her for eighty years - anchored off Gosport at Portsmouth. There are also, alas, many other poor postcards with little merit.

Victory enjoys about 350,000 visits a year and, during her life, must have been visited by people from almost every nation in the world. What many of them probably do not realise is that *Victory* was multi-national, particularly at Trafalgar. Apart from the 700 Englishmen, Irishmen, Scotsmen and Welshmen, there were 18 other nations represented in the crew, including 22 Americans. Included in this global company there were also Frenchmen, the enemy at the time.

68. The Cathedral of the Navy. HMS Victory, *Showing Stern. Tonnage 2162 Ton - publisher unknown*

The Cathedral of the Navy.   H.M.S. VICTORY, Showing Stern.   Tonnage 2162 Tons.

Victory is significant as it is one of the few associations with Nelson's life that we can still see and touch. It is the place where he died and its very name embodies Nelson's greatest aim. Described on this postcard as 'The Cathedral of the Navy', *Victory* is described on others as a 'Shrine' - it is indeed a place of hero-worship and regarded now as a national treasure. It was not always valued to that degree nor kept in the condition in which we can see it today.

The building of *Victory* began in 1759. She was eventually launched in 1765 at a cost of £97,400, but was then not needed so was not fitted out until 1778 when she first saw active service. She went through successive periods of service followed by refitting until 1797 when she was converted to a hospital ship. Following the failure of the Peace of Amiens and the outbreak of war in 1803, *Victory* was refitted again as a flagship for Nelson at a cost of £70,000. She underwent the next two years without docking until she needed major repair as a consequence of the damage she sustained at Trafalgar.

69. HMS Victory. *Nelson's Barge - published by Gale & Polden Ltd*

H.M.S. Victory. Nelson's Barge.

After a major refit, *Victory* then became flagship to Sir James Saumarez until 1812 and then languished with no proper rôle until 1823, when she became flagship of the Port Admiral at Portsmouth and permanently at anchor from 1842 off Gosport.

Victory's future was in the balance for years. She was something of a liability for an Admiralty that could only spend money on useful ships and in 1831, Thomas Hardy, as First Sea Lord, signed an order for her to be broken up. The story goes that his wife made him go back to his office and cancel the order.

Princess Victoria, then 16, and her mother, the Duchess of Kent, visited *Victory* two years later and, among other things, enjoyed a meal of beef and potatoes on a wooden platter. When, in June 1837, she ascended the throne as Queen Victoria, the first Royal Salute of 21 guns was fired by *Victory. Victory* also fired Queen Victoria's Coronation Salute. Returning to London from the Isle of Wight, Queen Victoria broke her journey to visit the ship. Later she arranged for the funeral barge in which Nelson made his last journey to be put on show aboard the ship. The Queen visited again with Prince Albert in 1844 when she noticed *Victory* bedecked with flags as she was on a visit to Portsmouth. Learning that it was Trafalgar Day, she insisted on going aboard and was visibly moved as she saw where Nelson had fallen and where he died.

70. HMS Victory *Dressed in Honour of HM Queen Victoria's Birthday - published by Sidney Smith, Fareham*

PHOTO BY   H.M.S. VICTORY.   SIDNEY SMITH FAREHAM.
DRESSED IN HONOR OF H.M.QUEEN VICTORIA'S BIRTHDAY

Many postcards can be found of *Victory* flying the Trafalgar signal or general bunting. Sidney Smith of Fareham, for instance, published this real photographic divided back postcard using a picture that must have been taken at least a few years earlier. The example in my collection was posted in 1933!

71. HMS Victory - *published by Raphael Tuck & Sons Ltd* Empire *postcard No. 598*

Victory also had the honour of firing the last salute when Queen Victoria's body passed by as it was being brought back from Osborne, Isle of Wight, after her death in 1901. During her reign, the Nelsonian traditions of celebrating Trafalgar Day, the drinking of the toast to the Immortal Memory and the flying of the 'England Expects' signal were established. Royal birthdays and significant events were also marked by *Victory* salutes. This postcard of *Victory* firing a salute is an undivided back card which means that it was probably published before 1902.

72. HMS Victory *The Upper Deck - published by Misch & Co* Nelson Centenary *Series no. 316/5*

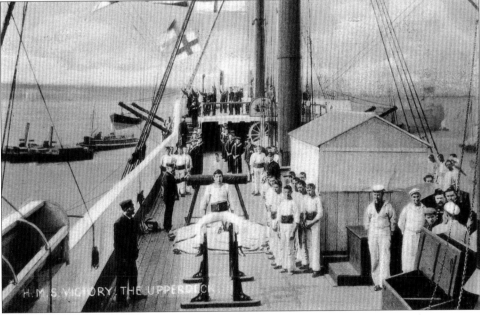

During her 1814 refit, *Victory*'s bow was remodelled, her waist decked over, her repaired fig-ure-head replaced and strengthening work done, including the fitting of iron knees. The great majority of early twentieth century postcards show *Victory* with this quite different profile.

As the twentieth century progressed, *Victory* changed to meet the needs of the crew of the time. Buildings appeared on deck, as can be seen in this postcard, and gun ports were con-verted to windows. The upper deck here is being used for crew gymnastics.

During this time, Nelson was not entirely forgotten. There was a collection of Nelson relics preserved on board as well as his funeral barge. Wherrymen were busily employed taking visitors from shore to ship and back again in their brightly coloured wherries. Just as today, not all of the ship was open to the public, but the quarterdeck bore the familiar plaque indi-cating the place where Nelson fell, and retired sailors were on hand to walk them round. It was, though, a lot more difficult to actually get on board as they had to climb a ladder.

Though Nelson's memory was preserved on *Victory,* the ship itself changed through the years that she was moored. She was kept in poor condition, with second-hand equipment used for repairs, and her timbers also deteriorated. In 1886, she had to be dry-docked to deal with woodworm. She was damaged significantly when *Neptune* rammed her on 23 October 1903.

Following repairs to *Victory*, Admiral Archibald Douglas flew his flag in her from 18 March 1905 to 1 March 1907, during which time the Trafalgar Centenary occurred and this post-card was published. The postcard, which is easily found, seems to have gone through several variable quality reprints, as the collector will note. That evidence of high sales level was not just the result of the interest in the Trafalgar Centenary and in Nelson, but was also partly due to the postcard collecting mania that swept the country at the time.

The state of *Victory* was becoming critical and by 1921 the President of the Society for Nautical Research reported that she was in real danger of sinking. She was moved into the old dockyard (No 2 Dry Dock) on 12 January 1922.

George V, on his way to join his yacht for a visit to the fleet, paid a visit and noted how low in the dock the *Victory* was. As a result, in three stages of lift, she was raised by April 1925 so that she gave the appearance of being afloat in her surrounding sea. On 25 April 1925, she left the water for the last time, eventually to sit on a stone base.

74. *Here Nelson Fell - published by Gale & Polden Ltd*

75. HMS Victory *In Dock - published by C. Cozens*

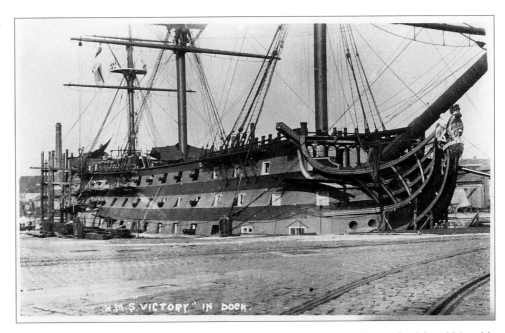

H.M.S. VICTORY IN DOCK.

This photographic postcard shows *Victory* in dock before being fully raised in 1925, with work going on around her gingerbreads (stern). Note how low she appears compared with later postcards, and particularly modern postcard views. Note also the window frames occupying the gun ports. The restoration costs were a huge problem.

The Cathedral of the Navy. H.M.S. VICTORY. Portsmouth Dockyard.
THE MOST FAMOUS SHIP PERMANENTLY RESTING IN THE SMALLEST AND OLDEST DOCK
IN THE WORLD. NOW RESTORED TO HER ORIGINAL CONDITION WHEN AT TRAFALGAR.
M & CO.   TONNAGE 2162 TONS.   No 140.

The Society for Nautical Research took on the job and had by 1932 raised £105,000 through the *Save the Victory* public appeal. As soon as £50,000 had been raised, work started. The aim was to restore the vessel to its 1805 specification but at the same time to safeguard its future. This was no small job, and it was with great pride that the work was completed in July 1928. This postcard echoes the feeling of the time.

King George V visited again on 17 July 1928 and expressed the gratitude of the nation for a job well done. He formally re-opened *Victory* to the public.

76.   HMS   Victory   - published by Misch & Co

77. Where Nelson Fell - published by Wright & Logan

Visitor interest has been constant and numbers have continually increased.

Work to restore and maintain *Victory* continues to this day - work which is monitored by the Victory Advisory Technical Committee. There have been set-backs since the work of restoration began. On the night of 10/11 March 1941, *Victory* was almost destroyed by the Germans. A 500lb bomb burst under the port bow and blew a hole in her hold 15 x 8ft wide. She also suffered a major attack by death-watch beetle in the 1960s but was saved.

Alongside *Victory* is the Portsmouth Royal Naval Museum, opened in 1898, and also a product of the Society's funding. WL Wyllie, whose panorama of Trafalgar can be seen there, also painted scenes for postcards.

This postcard shows *Victory's* fine figurehead which is a restoration of the figurehead dating from the 1801-1803 refit. This beautiful bow had been greatly altered by the creation of a tougher beak in the 1820s, ordered by Sir Robert Seppings, Surveyor to the Navy, which is evident in many postcards of the early part of the twentieth century.

Evidence found in the 1990s suggested that the two white cupids behind the Royal Coat of Arms were originally draped with different coloured material. The bands that wrap over their shoulders and around their waists are now coloured as they were at Trafalgar, red on the port side and blue on the starboard side. The colours indicate respectively a Seraphim, which is a higher-order angel representing love, and a Cherubim, a second-order angel representing wisdom. At Trafalgar, the starboard figure lost a leg while the port figure lost an arm.

78. HMS Victory. *"The Ship's Figurehead" - published by Photochrom Co. Ltd No. G5139*

H.M.S. VICTORY. "THE SHIP'S FIGUREHEAD"   G5139

79. HMS Victory. The Gingerbreads - publisher unknown no. V9

79. HMS Victory. *The Gingerbreads - publisher unknown no. V9*

V 9   H.M.S. "VICTORY". THE GINGERBREADS.

The stern of *Victory* (the gingerbreads), which at Trafalgar had carried a lot of carving and decoration, was restored between 1970 and 1978. At that time the stern was largely rebuilt from the keel to the poop deck.

Postcards record some of the changes. During the 1801-1803 refit, galleries - which were where the rows of pilasters are now - had been removed to create a flat stern. Study of postcards of *Victory's* stern when moored off Gosport show how much it had been changed in looks from its Trafalgar appearance.

H.M.S. VICTORY, THE DECK, SHOWING THE BOATS AND BELFRY   V678

This postcard shows some of *Victory's* boats stowed on skid beams set across the deck. Spare spars were similarly stowed. Before battle, the boats were put into the water and towed. This reduced their potential to become a source of dangerous splinters and made them available for message carrying, assisting sailors in the water and for wreckage clearing. *Victory* carried 6 boats - 1 launch, I barge, 1 pinnace and 3 cutters.

80. HMS Victory, *The Deck, Showing The Boats And Belfry - published by Photochrom & Co. Ltd no. V678*

81. *HMS* Victory, *The Masts, Rigging And Quarter Davits - published by Photochrom & Co. Ltd no. V13*

The complexity of the rigging of a ship such as *Victory* is evident in this postcard that shows just a small section of the full rig. The picture was obviously taken before the completion of the restoration as evidenced by the glazed gun ports. In all, about 26 miles of rope was used to rig the ship and hoist the maximum number of 37 sails that had an area of 6,510 square yards (5,500 square metres); 23 spare sails were also carried.

One sail used at Trafalgar still exists - the fore-topsail with an area of 400 square yards is the largest single *Victory*/Trafalgar relic. It has about 90 shot holes in it and, though rarely seen in public (it was last seen at the International Festival of the Sea in 1998), it should be on show for the Trafalgar Bicentenary.

H.M.S. VICTORY, THE MASTS, RIGGING AND QUARTER DAVITS   V13

82. *HMS* Victory. *The Quarter Deck looking aft - published by Gale & Polden Ltd no. E,No31/G&P/249*

Among the most common *Victory* postcards are those which show the quarterdeck, and in particular the area of the deck marked with a small brass plaque indicating where Nelson fell when shot. The plaque is almost central in this postcard view. That part of the deck is not original as the actual planking was moved below decks to the place where he died. A replacement wheel can be seen beyond the plaque and behind the binnacle housing. Earlier postcards should be compared with the modern reconstruction. They are now a record of some of the changes made to *Victory* that have since had to be undone.

Victory was Nelson's home for eighteen months until he spent a short time ashore just before he left for Trafalgar. Items of his personal furniture and belongings can be seen in museums and pictured on postcards, some of which are shown later in this book. Personal furniture was often designed to fold for several reasons - space saving, ease of transport and ease of clearing when readying the ship for battle.

The private rooms and spaces that Nelson used on *Victory* also feature on picture postcards - some modern postcards like the one here which also shows the other great cabin, Captain Hardy's (top right). Nelson's dining room (top left), day cabin (bottom left) and sleeping quarters (bottom right) complete the card. Nelson's swinging cot is also shown with replicas of the original drapes made by Emma Hamilton. For officers, their made-to-measure cots had a dual use - they could also serve as their coffins.

84. HMS Victory. *The Ward Room - published by Knight Brothers Knight Series no. 1451*

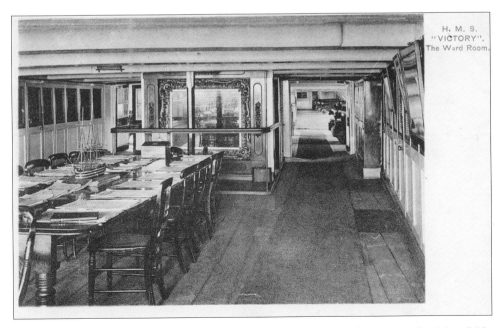

The wardroom was originally the officer's mess room. Cabins can be seen on the right of this postcard picture. In common with other parts of the ship, partitions could be removed together with the furniture before battle. Cannon can be seen in the background. The wardroom more recently served as a courtroom for any Portsmouth Port Command court martial.

85. Middle Gun Deck and Main Capstan - published by Hamilton-Fisher

Middle Gun Deck and Main Capstan

Apart from twenty-eight 24-pounder guns, the middle deck of *Victory* was where the upper part of the main capstan was situated.

This postcard shows the top of the capstan but without its removable conical top. When the top was removed, as in this picture, there was a flat space on which the ship's fiddler could sit and provide musical accompaniment for the 140 men needed to man the bars that slotted into the capstan drumhead.

When the bars were not in use, drawers that held wound dressings slotted into the spaces. When weighing anchor an extension trundlehead on the lower gun deck was also used. That required an additional 120 men on 12 bars, a total of 260 men. Ten tons could be lifted and, depending on the length of anchor cable that had been run out, raising anchor could take anything up to 6 hours.

86. HMS Victory *July 1928. Middle Deck & Officers Quarters - publisher unknown no. 17172*

This postcard picture of the Middle deck, taken at the time of the completion of the main restoration, shows officers' quarters and the capstan in the middle distance. It emphasises the lack of height (5ft) in the deck space, an area that in battle would have been filled with noise, smoke, traversing cannon balls and needle sharp splinters as well as blood. However, the sailor of Nelson's day would not, of course, have recognised the electrical conduits that can be seen in this picture attached to the deck beams.

87. HMS Victory 32 Pounder Guns, Lower Gun Deck - published by Gale & Polden Ltd no. E/No.10/G&P/53

This photographic view along the Lower gun deck reinforces the impressions given by the previous postcard. This deck was the heart of the ship. It was broader, more strongly built and 186 feet in length. Thirty 32-pounder guns, each weighing 3 tons, were housed here. Six men who lived, ate and slept amongst the guns formed a single gun crew. This deck was, therefore, home to 180 men. They were allowed just 20 inches of hammock space per man and, as they slept in their work clothes, both they and their beds were almost permanently wet.

88. HMS Victory, The Ship's Pumps - published by Photochrom Co. Ltd

H.M.S. VICTORY, THE SHIP'S PUMPS   V682

Every ship needed to be able to pump water out its bilges - the sump where waste and excess water collected as a result of leaks and waves washing onto the decks. This postcard shows *Victory's* main chain pump, the elm tree pump to its right and the main capstan trundlehead to the left with its 'messenger' cable that in turn helped to raise the main 24-inch anchor hawser.

The Cockpit. Here Nelson Died

Below the Lower gun deck, and so below the waterline of *Victory*, is a shrine to Nelson. This place, reproduced on many postcards, is carefully looked after, though the arrangement of pictures, wreaths and so forth has changed over the years.

This area during battle was a repository for the injured and dying, once described as a 'butcher's shambles'. Nelson died here three hours after being wounded. Though in pain and concerned for his loved ones, he was aware of the scope and significance of his achievement - an accomplishment which 200 years on we still find breathtaking.

Arthur Devis, who assisted at the autopsy, sketched both the area where Nelson died and those present at his end. Recent study of his sketches, inspired by a dogged determination to do full justice to Nelson by getting the story right, has led modern researchers to support the argument that Nelson actually died 25 feet further forward of the spot visited by millions of people and illustrated on thousands of postcards like this one.

Victory is a wonderful tribute to the dedication of Nelson enthusiasts in their pursuit of the accurate detail of the man and the events in which he played a central part. As more is learned, so *Victory* shall present an ever more accurate record.

Chapter Three
Pictures, Portraits, Models and Song

Nelson's life and achievements belonged, of course, to a time before the camera and photography made it possible to capture scenes and images of people accurately and then reproduce pictures at will. Drawings, etchings, paintings and sculpture were the precursors of the photograph and this is how Nelson's story was first pictorially presented to the public.

Fortunately, Nelson was a popular subject and was drawn and painted from about eighteen years of age by a variety of artists. Nelson's battles and, as he became famous, his earlier life became the subject of paintings, too. Trafalgar, the greatest battle and the event that marked the end of his life, was painted by many artists and is still painted today. The National Maritime Museum at Greenwich has a particularly good collection of Nelson-related paintings, but they can also be found in many major galleries.

Many of the major works of art relating to Nelson's life featured in the output of the various postcard publishers at some time. Both the battle of Trafalgar and Nelson's wounding and death, for example, feature often as themes. Modern postcards are carrying on this tradition so there are many postcards for the collector that reflect, as well as different scenes, differences of style, too. Postcards are themselves works of art but most in this section show reproductions of much larger paintings. Postcard collectors interested in building a collection of Nelson-related paintings on postcards should find ideas to start them off. Not all the postcard reproductions are good quality copies, though!

Of all the artists, Richard Westall's (1756-1831) work is probably most familiar to postcard collectors. He produced a series of paintings of incidents in the life of Nelson that were reproduced by a variety of postcard publishers early in the twentieth century. Many of these postcard pictures of Nelson were issued in sets or series.

I would emphasise that the content of this section represents only a glimpse at the total postcard output and that it highlights only a fraction of the works of art inspired by Nelson and his story. The sorts of postcard found in this section are, in fact, found throughout the book on other pages in other sections.

I have also included postcards featuring models and song as examples of the many other art forms. Perhaps they could give a focus to a different sort of Nelson collection.

It seems that Nelson is due for an image change as the result of new research by Dr Ann-Mary Hills, an expert on Nelson's health and wounds. Her work appears to explain why so many portraits, and therefore so many postcards, show Nelson from his left side. She contends that he had lost half of his right eyebrow at Calvi in 1794 and also suffered significant scarring to his forehead. This disfigurement was covered to a degree by Nelson's style of wearing his hair low down on his right forehead and was not evident in many pictures that were selectively angled to show him from his undamaged side. The pastel portrait of Nelson by Johann Heinrich Schmidt shown on a National Maritime Museum postcard in this chapter, seems in the light of this research to be, therefore, particularly accurate.

The Royal Naval Museum in Portsmouth has already operated on the right eyebrow of its waxwork figure of Nelson so perhaps the findings of Dr Hills may be reflected in future postcard output, too.

The portraits of Nelson by Lemuel Abbott (1760-1803) are probably the best-known Nelson paintings of all. Abbott painted Nelson, who gave two sittings at William Locker's house at Greenwich Hospital in Autumn 1797, when he was convalescing after the loss of his arm.

The original painting was subsequently re-worked about 40 times and versions can be seen in the National Portrait Gallery and the National Maritime Museum as well as elsewhere.

This postcard is a copy of the National Portrait Gallery version that belonged to Lady Nelson and was acquired in 1874 for £150.

The later versions, in which the real Nelson has all but disappeared, are probably better known and often appear in Nelson-related works. Evidence suggests, interestingly, that Nelson did not like the picture.

The first of the two leading ladies in the life of Nelson was Frances 'Fanny' Nisbet, the widowed daughter of the President of Nevis and owner of Montpelier plantation there.

The painter of this portrait is unknown but other images of Frances include a miniature by Samuel Shelley and a 1798 portrait by Daniel Orme. She was not a popular subject for the postcard publisher and, despite her importance in the Nelson story, seems to have been totally ignored in any series based on his life. This modern postcard is the only postcard of her that I have found.

91. *Frances, Viscountess Nelson 1761-1831 - published by the National Maritime Museum (copyright NMM)*

92. *Lady Hamilton by G. Romney - published by National Gallery/E. Wrench Ltd, The* Wrench *Series no. 840*

National Gallery
LONDON

Lady Hamilton
by
G. Romney

nelson's friend .

Emma Hart, later Emma Hamilton, was painted many times by George Romney who found her to be an excellent model, and another of Romney's pictures of her on postcard can be found earlier in the book.

As Emma Hart, she was the mistress of Charles Greville from 1782 and he passed her on to his uncle, Sir William Hamilton, in 1784 when he wanted her out of the way so that he could get married. During her time with Charles Greville, she met and sat for George Romney, who produced some of the finest examples of portraiture featuring her. Nelson preferred the pastel portrait by Johann Heinrich Schmidt (1749-1821) shown in an earlier part of the book, which is hardly surprising. Nevertheless, Nelson paid £300 (equivalent to £15,000) for a Romney portrait of Emma which had been put up for sale by Sir William. To maintain confidentiality the purchase was made on behalf of Nelson by his agent, Alexander Davison.

93. *The* Victory *Leaving Spithead, 1791 Robert Dodd, 1748-1815 - published by the National Maritime Museum no. 51 (copyright NMM)*

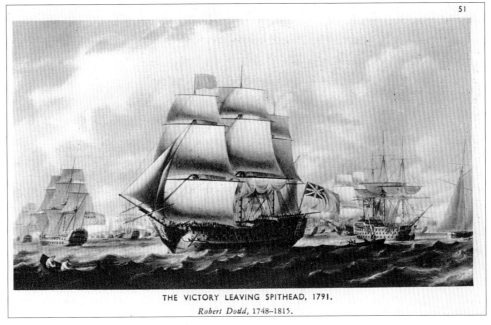

THE VICTORY LEAVING SPITHEAD, 1791.
Robert Dodd, 1748-1815.

This postcard shows an oil on canvas painting by Robert Dodd (1748-1816). It shows *Victory* earlier in her life, in 1791. The painting is currently in the National Maritime Museum, Greenwich. The ship had already seen action off Cape Ushant in 1778 and during the relief of Gibraltar in 1782, and is pictured here when she was the flagship of Lord Hood.

Dodd, an English marine painter, produced other work, including a painting of Nelson *Forcing the Passage of the Sound*, a prelude to the Battle of Copenhagen. This work could possibly be intended as a representation of the Royal Review on 1 July 1791, as ships in the background seem to be firing a salute.

94. Captain Horatio Nelson. 1758-1805 by John Francis Rigaud - published by the National Maritime Museum (copyright NMM)

This is the earliest authenticated portrait of Horatio Nelson. Rigaud began the three-quarter length oil portrait that appears here on a National Maritime Museum postcard when Nelson was an eighteen-year-old lieutenant. The picture had been commissioned by William Locker, captain of the *Lowestoffe*. Riguad completed it four years later when Nelson returned from the West Indies in 1781.

Because of Nelson's promotion, the artist had by then to alter several parts of the picture. Nelson was ill with Yellow Jack fever and commented *"It will not be in the least like I am now, that is certain, but you may tell Mr Rigaud to add beauty, and it will be much mended"*.

In the uncompleted picture, Nelson held his hat under his left arm. It was repositioned and placed on his head. His uniform was brought up to date and the fortress of San Juan in Nicaragua, which Nelson had helped to capture, placed in the picture.

The original picture was kept by Locker until 1800 when he bequeathed it to William, Horatio's brother. It remained in Nelson's family until 1947.

Henry Edridge, (1769-1821) worked from a studio in Bloomsbury close to Nelson's Old Bond Street address. He first painted Nelson in 1797. This postcard copy of a watercolour in the National Portrait Gallery shows a later picture of Nelson wearing all his decorations. He is portrayed with a rounder face - almost a Bonaparte look-alike. Careful study of the upper part of Nelson's right sleeve reveals what appear to be ribbons. These closed a purpose-made cut in the sleeve that could be opened to allow him to be assisted in working his right arm stump into the top of the sleeve.

95. Portrait of Nelson from Painting In National Portrait Gallery - published by Gottschalk, Dreyfus & Davis, The Star Series

NELSON 1801.

96. *Nelson 1801 - publisher unknown (Pictorial Post Card)*

Collectors should have little trouble finding a copy of this postcard as it, too, was popular and copies still turn up regularly in dealers' boxes. The original painting was the Lemuel Abbott portrait.

John McArthur, former Secretary to Lord Hood, who knew Nelson, commissioned a variation of Abbott's portrait as an illustration for *The Naval Chronicle* in 1799. Abbott added the tricorn hat with its prominent chelengk decoration. The fabulous chelengk had been a gift from the Sultan of Turkey.

As easily the most popular portrait of Nelson, it was reproduced in various forms and with various titles by a large percentage of postcard publishers. It remains popular and is usually found among the modern postcard selections on offer at maritime and Nelson museums today. The quality of reproduction is, though, significantly better!

This postcard shows one of the two masks of Nelson's face, which were made from casts moulded in Vienna in 1800 when he was travelling back to England overland through Europe.

The sculptor, Franz Thaller, wanted to make a bust of the tremendously popular Nelson but as time was limited Nelson allowed Matthias Ranson to make a cast of his face for Thaller's use.

For many years the Nelson masks were thought to have been made post mortem. More recently, they have become accepted as true likenesses of a living Nelson. The various portraits of the hero have also been re-evaluated.

97. *Face of a Hero - published by the National Maritime Museum (copyright NMM)*

98. Nelson - published by the National Maritime Museum (copyright NMM)

This fine postcard picture of Nelson was painted by Johann Heinrich Schmidt. Schmidt was the Court painter at Dresden to which Nelson and his party travelled after their stays in Vienna and Prague while on the way back to England.

This pastel portrait is the companion to the one of Emma Hamilton that Nelson kept with him. Although not the most flattering of pictures, it probably is amongst the most honest, showing a face damaged by war wounds and stressed by his personal problems. The portrayal of Nelson's facial wounds and of the damage to his right eye, dating back to Calvi in 1794, are particularly significant in the light of the recent research by Dr Ann-Mary Hills referred to in the introduction to this chapter.

John Hoppner (1758-1810) was commissioned to paint a portrait of Nelson by the Prince of Wales, who wanted a picture of Nelson for Carlton House. This portrait was also destined to be copied many times. The original, completed before 1802, shows the Battle of Copenhagen in the background. After Nelson's death, when the picture was reworked, the Battle of Trafalgar was substituted. The Prince of Wales, incidentally, received his picture, after quite a long wait, in 1810. Apparently he had been reluctant to pay.

99. Lord Nelson - published by J Salmon Ltd no. 15-58-04-53

100. Nelson In His Cabin - published by Knight Brothers, Knight Series no. 1448

This postcard shows a portrait in oils of Nelson in the Great Cabin of *Victory* on the morning of 21 October 1805. It is by Charles Lucy and can be found reproduced by several different postcard publishers. Nelson's friends thought it one of the most life-like, though it was not painted until 1853, 48 years after Nelson's death.

Unlike the obviously posed portraits, it shows Nelson in contemplative mood, having just written the famous codicil to his will. This postcard version has an inset showing Nelson's famous Prayer Before Battle.

101. The Battle of Trafalgar - published by National Maritime Museum (copyright NMM)

As might be expected, Nelson's battles and involvement in heroic action were favourite subjects for the artist and equally popular images for the postcard publisher. The postcards would certainly constitute an interesting Nelson collection too large for this section. With limited space, the images included here are only those of Nelson's most famous battle, Trafalgar.

This postcard, from the National Maritime Museum, is a modern card showing *The Battle of Trafalgar* as painted by Joseph Mallord William Turner, (1775-1851).

The caption tells us that it was '*Turner's only royal commission, ordered by George IV in 1822*' and that it '*combines a series of incidents into an evocation of events which displeased most naval officers and proved highly controversial when it was delivered in 1822 ...*' It was the largest picture ever painted by Turner, who spent 11 days correcting errors which had been noted when it went on view. Even so, *Victory* is seen flying part of the '*England Expects ...*' signal, a mid-day event, while her top mizzen-mast is down, a 1pm event. The picture also shows *Redoutable* sinking, which did not happen there during the battle, but the next day and somewhere else.

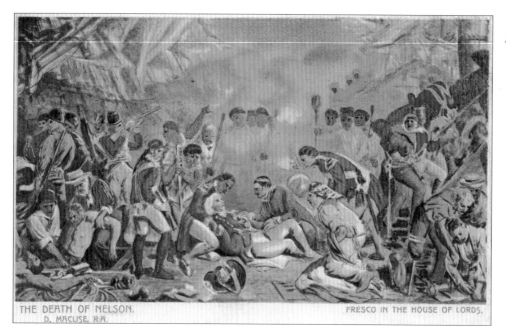

THE DEATH OF NELSON.
D. MACLISE, R.A.

FRESCO IN THE HOUSE OF LORDS.

The scene on this postcard is taken from a much larger work - a huge mural or fresco in the Palace of Westminster Royal Gallery, entitled *Trafalgar: The Death of Nelson*. It is the work of Daniel Maclise, (1811-1870), and though not historically accurate, as it shows Nelson dying on the quarterdeck of *Victory* rather than in the cockpit of the ship, it is superbly detailed. Unfortunately, that quality is lost in the postcard reproduction, which is crudely printed.

This postcard portrayal of the death of Nelson, painted in 1806, is reproduced from an oil on canvas painting by the American-born Benjamin West (1738-1820). West became George III's royal history painter and was a co-founder of the Royal Academy, of which he

N 5 ROTARY PHOTO. E.C.

DEATH OF NELSON

became President in 1792. It was at this time that Nelson met him.

Nelson admired West's painting of the death of Wolfe, and West answered Nelson's query as to why he had not painted others of that theme by explaining that there was a lack of subject matter. West suggested that Nelson might one day provide him with another such scene if he carried on taking the risks that he was famed for. Nelson was delighted and said *"Will you, Mr West? Then I hope I shall die in the next battle!"*

The picture, intended to be an epic scene in the Renaissance tradition, shows Nelson just after having been shot, with many of the individual portraits supposedly having been taken from life. Like Maclise's painting reproduced on the previous postcard, it suggests that he died on the quarterdeck. It was popular when first shown and top of the best sellers list when sold as a print. It is, though, to the modern critic, rather static and gives the impression of a posed scene.

West, incidentally, fell out of favour with his royal sponsor after praising Napoleon Bonaparte and visiting Paris in 1802.

104. *The Death Of Nelson - published by Misch & Co. The* Great Masters *Series no. 442*

This early twentieth century postcard shows another of Joseph Mallord William Turner's paintings of the Trafalgar battle. He has used a different viewpoint here - more a bird's eye view. Although the postcard is entitled *The Death of Nelson* it is catalogued as *The Battle of Trafalgar, as seen from the Mizen Starboard Shrouds of The Victory* (sic).

The picture can now be seen in the Tate Gallery. The postcard does the painting no justice but it is typical of many poorly reproduced postcards that were put on sale to cash in on the collecting craze of the time.

105. *Death Of Nelson In The Cockpit Of The* Victory - *published by E Wrench Ltd , The* Wrench *Series no. 10502*

This painting by Arthur William Devis was 9 feet long. It has been reproduced on many different postcards. The colour reproductions of the earlier twentieth century postcards were made without benefit of modern techniques and are not as sharp as this monochrome card.

Devis worked as assistant to Sir William Beatty, who performed the autopsy on Nelson. Devis also worked as the equivalent of the modern forensic photographer, sketching the body, scene, and those who were present at the death. As a result, his work had an accuracy unmatched and his portrayal, with its likeness to a Renaissance religious scene, underlined the parallel which rapidly emerged between the death of Nelson and that of one of God's chosen heroes.

106. Lord Viscount Nelson K.B. - published by Excelsior Fine Arts Co Ltd (J Arthur Dixon), Nelson Series no. 565

Lord Viscount Nelson K. B.

The unusual portrait reproduced on this postcard was also the work of Arthur Devis. He produced it using the sketches he had made during the autopsy. He shows Nelson using an eye-shade, which he had incorporated in his hat. The design for this still exists in the records of James Lock's shop in London, from whom Nelson bought the original.

This unusual postcard is included as an example of artistic licence. Its creator is unknown. Nelson did have an eye shade built into his hat to protect him from excessively bright light, as can be seen in the Devis picture on the previous postcard. His damaged eye was almost normal to look at and, though he could only distinguish light and dark, there is no record of him ever having worn an eye patch. The card exemplifies a common misconception about Nelson. This image and other similar efforts can only have come from confusion with some piratical image.

107. Admiral Lord Nelson 1758-1805 - published by W.N. Sharpe Ltd, Classic All British Series no. 26, Card no. 226

Effigy of
Lord Nelson
1805

108. *Effigy of Lord Nelson 1805 - published by Lovering & Co.*

The wax and wood effigy of Nelson that was commissioned for Westminster Abbey after Nelson's death can be found reproduced on postcards from a variety of publishers. The figure itself was the work of Catherine Andras for whom Nelson had sat. Though she used that previous knowledge of him, the pose of the figure is very similar to that of Hoppner's portrait for the Prince of Wales. The end result was very lifelike, impressing everyone and particularly Emma, Lady Hamilton, who said *"the general carriage was exactly his, and altogether the likeness was so great it was impossible for anyone who had known him to doubt or mistake it"*.

This oddly coloured postcard shows the work of an art prodigy, John Everett Millais (1829-1896) who entered the Royal Academy Schools at the age of 11. With Hunt and Rossetti he founded the Pre-Raphaelite Brotherhood in 1848. His choice of Greenwich Pensioners was deliberate. They, together with *Victory*'s crew and officers, walked in Nelson's funeral procession.

GREENWICH PENSIONERS AT THE TOMB OF NELSON.
From the picture by Sir John E. Millais, Bart., P.R.A.

"Cassell's Saturday Journal" Postcards

109. *Greenwich Pensioners At The Tomb Of Nelson - published by Cassell & Co. Ltd* Cassell's Saturday Journal *Postcards*

From a later era, William Lionel Wyllie (1851-1931) displayed an almost photographic ability as an artist and is numbered amongst the greatest *Victory* artists.

Postcards of his work have steadily increased in value and, because of their quality, it is easy to understand why. Wyllie worked for the White Star Shipping Line as well as the Royal Navy and the Royal Naval Museum at Portsmouth has many of his paintings.

John Fry's work has, for similar reasons, marked him out as 'collectable'. He, too, is very detailed, and has a three-dimensional quality that is promoted by the mock oil painting nature of the production of this card. This postcard of *Victory* is one of three different views of the scene painted by Fry and featuring on Salmon postcards that I know of, though there could be others.

111. The Victory, *Portsmouth - published by J Salmon Ltd, no. 3443*

112. Detailed Model of Buckler's Hard Village in 1803, Maritime Museum, Buckler's Hard, Hampshire - published by Pitkin Pictorials Ltd no. BUC 14

Model-making has its part to play in preserving and promoting the story of Nelson, and it is appropriate to look at this model of Bucklers Hard, which tells us so much about how Nelson's ships were built. The wonderful model shown on this modern postcard is on view in the excellent Bucklers Hard Museum, along with other Nelson memorabilia, including his baby clothes. The model shows Bucklers Hard as it was during the building of *Swiftsure* and *Euryalus*, with *Euryalus* ready for launching. *Agamemnon*, believed to be Nelson's favourite ship, was built here, too, and together with *Swiftsure* and *Euryalus* fought at Trafalgar *(see also illus. 146)*.

H.M.S. Victory

This modern postcard shows one of the most popular of all ship models - *Victory*. It is also one of the most difficult to make and models such as this take a long time to build. This particular model, made by B Hollinshead, took nine years. It is now in the Nelson Collection at Monmouth. The copper plating, we are told on the reverse of the card, is held by 20,000 hand made miniature nails.

Another modeller spent 3,500 hours spread over six years on his *Victory* model and no doubt there are many other *Victory* builders to be found around the world.

113.   HMS   Victory, Monmouth   Museum - published by Conrad

114. Model Of The HMS Lord Nelson *On Regatta Day - 1913 - publisher unknown*

This postcard has particular charm and interest because it shows the Navy at play in 1913, just before the outbreak of World War I. The model of HMS *Lord Nelson*, the only battleship to bear that version of Nelson's name, is sailing past another anchored model. Is it HMS *Iron Duke*?

115. Navy Week Portsmouth - published by Stephen Cribb, Southsea

The large-scale sailing model, *Victory II,* was built in 1930 in Portsmouth, probably in the Gunboat Yard, Haslar Creek, Gosport. She was built as the result of an idea of Captain GE Boultbee, then on the staff of Admiral Sir Roger Keys, the Commander in Chief, Portsmouth.

At the heart of the model was a 42-foot launch around which was built the *Victory* bodywork. A Buick starter motor, powered by batteries, was used to help turn the model. The crew fired Very pistols through the gun ports to simulate a broadside, and the early model was intended to sail only within the dockyard basin. During Navy Week in 1930 sail drill demonstrations were given. In 1931, the model was completely planked-in so that it became seaworthy. She was manned by sailors from HMS *Hood* and cruised in the Channel and up the Thames to the Houses of Parliament. Postcards featuring that voyage and other appearances of the model make a fascinating collection.

116. *"The miniature model of Nelson's famous flagship,* Victory.... *the modern giant* Nelson" ... *- published by Raphael Tuck & Sons*

Victory II was also present at the Fleet Review at Spithead on 6 May 1935, attended by George V. This postcard shows the model alongside the battleship HMS *Nelson*, a flagship in its own right. A similar postcard can be found of *Victory II* with Nelson's sister ship, HMS *Rodney*. *Victory II* was laid up during the Second World War and, having deteriorated, was subsequently broken up.

117. *Twas in Trafalgar's bay.... - published by Birn Bros, London* Trafalgar *Series no. 296*

Twas in Trafalgar's bay
We saw the Frenchmen lay,
Each heart was bounding then,
We scorned the foreign yoke,
For our ships were british oak,
And hearts of oak our men

Nelson's exploits were also remembered in song. This postcard is one of a series of six featuring verses from the song *The Death of Nelson*.

The publisher, P Jones, issued a postcard *Souvenir of Nelson* with an 'additional verse' as a Trafalgar Centenary offering in 1905.

118. *The Death Of Nelson - publisher unknown no. 18/3A*

The melody for the *The Death of Nelson*, some lines of which feature on this card, was written in 1811 by the famous tenor, John Braham. The music came from his opera *The Americans*, first performed in 1811 at the Lyceum. Braham collaborated with S.J. Arnold in setting the music to the words. The addition of the particular words, '*this day*', to Nelson's 'England Expects …' signal is attributed to Arnold who presumably added them in order to make the words fit the music. He thus gave birth to a frequently met misquotation.

119. *Heart of Oak - published by Reid Bros. Ltd, London*

Postcards can readily be found featuring many other patriotic songs either directly mentioning Nelson or alluding to his example and tradition. This card sets the words of *Heart of Oak* alongside a picture of *Victory* moored at Portsmouth, making the intended association between the two very obvious.

120. *Rule Britannia (1) - published by Bamforth & Co. Ltd,* Holmfirth *Series no. 4775/1*

In a similar way, this postcard, which is one of a set, associates the first verse of *Rule Britannia* with Nelson. It seems to be the odd one out in the set. The person who planned the series apparently could not think of any other nautical heroes, as other cards in this set feature early twentieth century battleships.

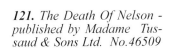

RULE, BRITANNIA (1).

When Britain first, at Heaven's command,
Arose from out the azure main,
This was the charter of the land,
And guardian angels sang this strain:

121. *The Death Of Nelson - published by Madame Tussaud & Sons Ltd. No.46509*

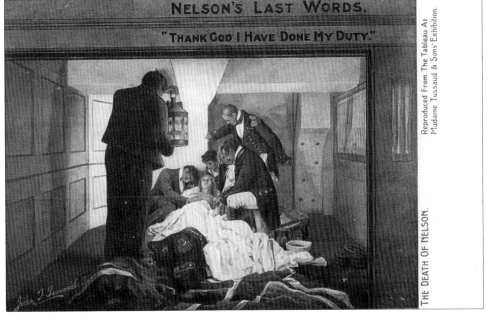

Madam Tussaud and Sons, famous for their wax works, naturally wished to have a Nelson exhibit. Here it is captured on postcard. The modelling of the scene for *The Death of Nelson* is taken from the painting by Arthur Devis, though only the main figures are included. The Madame Tussaud's *Trafalgar Experience* was open to the public until 1992.

The postcard was produced in at least two different versions. Another version has the caption down the left-hand side. Though the cards turn up from time to time, they are usually not in good condition. Madam Tussaud also published four cards in a *Battle of Trafalgar - as it happened* series. These are harder to find.

122. Figurehead of Lord Nelson - publisher unknown

Figureheads of Horatio Nelson took pride of place on a range of wooden ships, both naval and merchant, in the period between his death and the advent of the iron ship. Some have survived, such as the figurehead from HMS *Lion* which is at Portsmouth, the HMS *Boscawen* figurehead featured later in the book and the figurehead from the wooden HMS *Nelson* launched in 1814 which is now in the Sydney National Maritime Museum where it has had major restorative work.

The figurehead featured on this postcard was made for HMS *Vanguard* in 1835. While stored in Chatham Dockyard it was almost totally destroyed by fire in 1966. The face, which is all that remains, is displayed in the Chatham local Fire Brigade Headquarters.

Chapter Four
Statues, Columns, Towers and Plaques

Within a short time of Nelson's death, monuments were raised in his memory, and that process continued through much of the rest of the nineteenth century. In some cases, these were statues on plinths, in other cases tall columns decorated with scenes of his victories. Some were simple, like the prehistoric twelve-foot high granite pillar from Airds Bay, which was dragged on rollers to a new position in Taynuilt by the Lorn Furnace workmen who added an inscription. This was a memorial from the men who made cannon balls for the Fleet.

Nelson's friends, and those who served with him, were directly involved in subscribing to and dedicating memorials. Alexander Davison, Nelson's friend and agent, apart from the creation of a 100-acre Battle Park at his home at Swarland, Northumberland in celebration of the Battle of the Nile, erected a 40-foot obelisk in honour of Nelson close to the, then, Great North Road which ran past his estate.

Some monuments were representational while others were allegorical. Some parts of Britain and the world chose to remember Nelson by erecting special towers or buildings. Some were satisfied with a two-dimensional plaque. Good designers and sculptors found ample scope for their imagination and skills.

The world has a great legacy of Nelson memorials as a result - many of them in Britain. To date no single publisher has published a set of postcards solely recording statues or monuments dedicated to Nelson. Though most, if not all, of these structures appear on postcards, the cards are the work of a variety of publishers rather than of one. Valentine & Sons probably top the list, not because of a specific intention to feature Nelson but because their extensive coverage of all-important topographical and popular features resulted in the production of postcards of Nelson sites.

Tracking down postcards of all of the statues and monuments, or the publishing of a complete set, would be a nice project for Nelson's bicentenary. If anyone feels like taking up the challenge, the National Maritime Museum lists the major Maritime Memorials and 30 are listed for Horatio Nelson (two are shared with others).

Many of the 30 have already featured on postcards over the years and in this section I have presented a selection only, including the Dublin statue that was destroyed in 1966. Other memorials, such as the Barbados statue and the Kymin, appear elsewhere in the book. Most of these, and similar examples, should be found fairly readily by anyone setting out to build a collection, but there are the more difficult ones to find, too - the early cards and the centenary scenes in particular.

123. Photo of Original Bust (by Sir Edgar Boehm) on top of the 'Nelson' Column, Portsdown Hill - publisher unknown no. 974

The Nelson Monument sited on the top of Portsdown Hill at Portsmouth was a tribute to Nelson by his own Trafalgar Officers, Seamen and Marines. Postcards of the monument are hard to find. This real photographic card shows the bust of Nelson that is set into the very top of the column, a square-sectioned tapering pillar, 110 feet (36.5m) high. The column, designed by JT Grove, was begun in 1807, financed by the contribution of two day's pay by the men. It is the oldest monument to Nelson in the world. Nelson's column in London came 30 years later.

The Portsdown Memorial has recently been renovated at a cost of £30,000. Hopefully this will encourage a revival of the Trafalgar wreath-laying ceremony that used to be held there, and the publication of some postcards featuring the column.

£6,300 was set aside to provide a monument to Nelson in St Paul's Cathedral with the design made the subject of a competition. John Flaxman won but, strangely, only on condition that he used a rival's design. He took 12 years to complete the job.

John Flaxman had been introduced to Nelson by Sir William Hamilton, who told Nelson that Flaxman was the man who should make his monument. Nelson reportedly replied, *"then I heartily wish he may"*.

One anonymously-published postcard had the following description of the monument, which was erected in 1818: 'Britannia pointing her sons to one whose last utterance was a call to every man to do his duty'. The 'sons' are elsewhere more closely defined as midshipmen.

124. The Nelson Monument in St Paul's Cathedral - published by Gottschalk, Dreyfus & Davis, The Star Series

Nelson Monument, Calton Hill   Edinburgh

125. Nelson Monument, Calton Hill, Edinburgh - published by Stengel & Co.

Edinburgh's memorial had its foundation stone laid down in 1807, but then shortage of money delayed its completion. The design of the 106-foot Calton Hill Tower of five storeys was the brainchild of architect Robert Burn. It was intended to be useful as well as ornamental, and it has long been suggested that the inspiration was a telescope.

Caretakers were to be invalided seamen and the public could climb the 170 steps to view Edinburgh from a height. It served as a landmark for sailors, 456 feet above sea level, and from 1852 as an indicator of official time, when a mechanical signal was placed at the top. This was in the form of a ball that dropped down a short mark at 12 noon.

The Tower of Forres is remote. On the coast of Morayshire, 25 miles from Inverness, it is a 70-foot (21m) octagonal tower that was built in 1806 by the local *Trafalgar Club* to the design of Charles Stuart.

It stands on top of Cluny Hill and has three floors, 24 feet in diameter, with a viewing platform on top which looks out on to the Moray Firth and the Grampian mountains. It fell into disrepair in the latter half of the nineteenth century but is now restored.

126. Nelsons Tower, Forres - published by J Valentine & Sons Ltd no. 20102

127. Nelson's Monument, Liverpool - published by E Wrench Ltd. The Wrench Series no. 3196

The Liverpool monument was also arrived at through public competition. The result caused great local controversy as local artists were overlooked in favour of the sculptor Westmacott, who was involved with the St Paul's monument, the Birmingham monument in the Bull Ring, and a statue in Bridgetown, Barbados.

The winning Birmingham design was actually by Matthew Coates Wyatt. The monument tells the allegorical story of death claiming the hero. Made of Westmorland marble and of bronze, it has a circular pedestal with four emblematic captive and defeated figures arranged around the base.

128. Hereford, Cathedral and Castle Green - published by C Baker, Hereford

This postcard shows one of the less well-known memorials to Nelson, in Castle Green in Hereford. Hereford had a committee in charge of choosing a fitting memorial and, rather than pay 100 guineas for a statue of the great man, it opted for a column that could be afforded within the budget.

The resultant column is surmounted by an urn with a trophy and carries a Trafalgar inscription. A bust in relief was carved on the south side. The committee did move relatively quickly, though, as work began in March 1806, the column being erected in 1809. Much vandalised in recent years, the column is to be restored and more effectively protected by a security fence in future.

Many of the major cities and towns raised their unique memorials. This postcard shows the Birmingham monument in the Bull Ring. Westmacott was again the choice of sculptor, and his work was to be the first public monument in Birmingham, a place that was home to a powerful anti-war Quaker lobby. It was completed in 1809 and remained in place until the redevelopment of the area in 1959, when it was re-sited close by. A local auctioneer, Joseph Farrar, left 6d (2½ pence) in his will for it to be regularly cleaned. During the reconstruction of the Bull Ring area in 2001 it was put into storage. It was reinstated in September 2003, after renovation, as a central feature of a new £400 million pedestrianised Bull Ring.

Norwich lost out in the bid to become the home of the Norfolk monument, which was eventually built in Great Yarmouth. It did, nevertheless, in 1847, get its own statue that was erected in front of the Grammar School in the Cathedral Close. The sculpture, which cost 700 guineas, was the work of Thomas Milnes. The nine-foot figure was cut from a block of finest Sicilian marble. It was first erected in the Market Place opposite the entrance to Dove Street, but 18 months later it was moved to the Cathedral Close. It underwent renovation, paid for by a private benefactor, and was unveiled again on 13 May 2000.

130. Nelson's Centenary, Lord Nelson's Monument, Norwich - published by The Great Eastern Railway Series 1905

NELSON'S MONUMENT AND TUBULAR BRIDGE,
LLANFAIRPWLLGWYNGYLLGOGERYCHWYRNDROBWLL-LLANDYSLLIOGOGOGOCH

131. Nelson's Monument and Tubular Bridge Llanfairpwllgwyngyllgogerychwyrndrobwll-llandyslliogogogoch - published by J. Valentine & Sons Ltd no. 203775

Nelson statues and pillars sprang up all over the British Isles, and the postcard collector has a challenge trying to build a collection of all of them. This one is surely in the place with the longest name!

Designed by Clarence Paget, the Nelson memorial was sited on the banks of the Menai Strait, west of the Britannia Bridge in Anglesey, as an aide to navigation and was unveiled in 1873. The base, which is a square stone tower, has a ladder inside leading to a walkway around the 9-foot octagonal stone second level that supports the statue of Nelson.

132. The Cascade, Corby Castle, near Carlisle - publisher unknown

Some memorials are relatively secluded. This statue is in the grounds of Cosby Castle, near Carlisle. It is life size and stands beside a bridge close to the Capital Cascade. Made of coade stone, an artificial material, it is similar to the monument erected in 1808 in Montreal, Canada.

133. Nelson Pillar, Dublin - published by Eason & Son Ltd, Dublin & Belfast, Signal *Series*

The story of the memorial in Dublin is less happy. It was erected in what was then Sackville Street (now O'Connell Street) to the annoyance of republicans. A statue of Nelson stood on top of a pillar 103 feet high until 1966, when on 8 March, the 50th anniversary of the Easter Rising, the Irish Republican Army blew it up.

Many postcards can still be found showing how it dominated the area. The remains of the pillar and Nelson's statue are now long gone.

134. Nelson's Monument, Great Yarmouth - publisher unknown

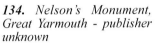

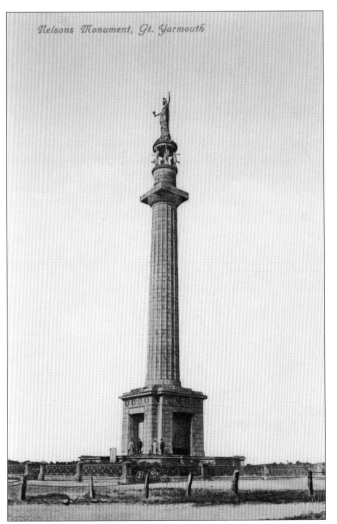

Nelson was proud of being a Norfolk man and, naturally, his home county wanted a fitting memorial to him. A site could not be agreed, even though, by 1806, over £800 had been collected. Nothing happened until 1815, when Great Yarmouth, a coastal site, was chosen. As was the case in other coastal areas, the monument was to be a navigational aide, too. William Wilkins, who had designed the Dublin memorial, was commissioned to build a column surmounted by Britannia. Many believed that a statue of Nelson should have been placed at the top, but Britannia was at least an improvement on the first proposal, a Roman galley!

The column, seen on this card and pictured on many others, was built on the South Denes in the centre of Great Yarmouth's original racecourse. Completed in 1819, the 144-foot hollow pillar (one foot shorter than the later Trafalgar Square column) could be climbed using the 217 steps so that a sea view could be enjoyed. The names of Nelson's victories and ships are on the sides of the pedestal and capital. James Sherman, who had served on *Victory,* was installed in a cottage close by as a caretaker. He gained fame by rescuing a crewman from the brig *Hammond* in 1829, after it was wrecked on the beach. As a consequence, Sherman became the inspiration for Charles Dickens' character of Ham Peggotty in David Copperfield.

Folklore has it that the architect jumped off the top: he did not. One man fell off the top, though, in 1863 - an acrobat by the name of Marsh who had succeeded in getting onto Britannia's shoulders but fell getting back down.

A Heritage Lottery Fund grant of approximately £850,000 will help restore the column in time for the Trafalgar Bicentenary in 2005. Closed for safety reasons in 1996, the internal staircase will be restored and a heritage officer employed.

Though the granite obelisk on Portsdown Hill, overlooking Portsmouth Harbour, was unique in being paid for by the Trafalgar Officers and men, this early undivided back postcard, posted in July 1901, shows the most famous statue of all - Nelson's Column in Trafalgar Square. This was intended

135. Trafalgar Square London - published by PVK Editions Cartes Postales Kunzli, Zurich no. 6158

to be a national monument and the site eventually chosen was the square in front of the National Gallery.

As with many other memorial ventures, the design for the London statue was made the subject of a competition with funding by subscription. William Railton won the commission with his design for a column to be topped with a 17-foot statue. The inspiration came from the temple of Mars Ultor and Trajan's Column in Rome. Fourteen select subscribers enjoyed a banquet on top of the column on 23 October 1843 before the statue was put in place. The likeness of Nelson had been designed by Edward Hodges Baily. Bas-reliefs of Nelson's victories, cast in bronze from captured enemy guns, were added to the base in 1854 (more about these elsewhere in the book) and the four great bronze guardian lions, designed by Landseer and sculpted by Baron Marochetti, were added in 1867.

When work began in 1840, Charles Davidson Scott laid the foundation stone. He was the youngest son of Nelson's secretary, John Scott, who was killed at Trafalgar minutes before Nelson himself was fatally wounded. The column, over 56 metres (185 feet) high, was sculpted from granite taken from Foggintor Quarry in Devon.

136. Nelson's Monument, Montreal - published by The Valentine & Sons Publishing Co., Montreal no. 106,139

United Kingdom geographical distances are measured from Trafalgar Square, which has become the focal point of visits to London, marches, meetings and the New Year celebrations. It has also been a focal point of anniversaries, the most important of which, for Nelson disciples, was the 1905 centenary of the Battle of Trafalgar, pictured later in the book. It is the essential place to be for celebrating any historic event, and if there is such a place as the heart of the nation then this is it.

The news of the Battle of Trafalgar reached Montreal, Canada, via a New York newspaper, which was brought into an Assembly Ball at Exchange House by a waiter. It was immediately decided that a monument should be erected. A coade stone statue was commissioned from the Lambeth, London firm of Coade and Seeley and was erected on a 50-foot column in the city in 1809.

The design was that of London architect Robert Mitchell and Joseph Panzetta. Engraved tablets depicting the Nelson battles were removed in 1900 and are now in the Château Ramezay. They were replaced with granite copies. The statue in the Place Jacques Cartier is in the 'Old City' and, though attempts were made in recent times to have it removed, it was restored in 1980. In 1999, a Toronto artist, Lawrence Cajban, was commissioned to make a replica statue in Indiana limestone that has since replaced the original.

What made the erection of a statue in Montreal unusual was that Montreal was historically predominantly French-speaking. On the back of my copy of this postcard is a surprising note. It relates how *'the officers of the garrison started a subscription. French as well as English gave liberally'*.

Nelson's Monument, Montreal   (First Monument erected to the Memory of Nelson)

137. Allegorical Carving, The Death of Nelson - publisher unknown

This postcard is of an unidentified panel, carved by a sailor in 1806 - evidence that not only professionals were involved in artistic efforts to remember Nelson. I haven't yet been able to find out where it is or whose work it may have been.

138. Nelson Memorial, Town Hall, Pontefract - published by Oswald Holmes, Advertiser Office, Pontefract

This postcard shows a large (approximately 20-foot square) panel on the wall of the Moot (Town) Hall at Pontefract, in the West Riding of Yorkshire. It was the work of IE Carew and served as a model for one of the bas-reliefs at the base of Nelson's Column in Trafalgar Square. It was originally placed in the Board of Works. It survived threat of destruction in 1857 and was acquired by the Corporation in November 1905, the Trafalgar Centenary year. Believing it was a gift to the people of Pontefract, the Corporation was surprised to receive a bill for £500.

139. HMS Boscawen *1841-1905 - publisher unknown*

Of all the likenesses produced after his death, Nelson would, probably, have been most proud of the various figureheads which graced Royal Navy ships until wooden ships were superseded.

This figurehead originally belonged to HMS *Trafalgar*, launched in 1841. At the end of her service life she replaced the training ship for boy seamen, HMS *Boscawen*, at Portland and was re-named. At the end of her life in 1905 she was sold, but the figurehead was saved and eventually displayed near HMS *Victory*.

Chapter Five
Memorabilia, the Nelson name and Association

Any collector choosing to concentrate on postcards of this type has a wide choice available. Almost every town and city in Britain has its Nelson streets, squares, parks, public houses and hotels. Similarly, so do innumerable places around the world. The process began while Nelson was alive. He allegedly heard that the *Wrestler's Inn* at Great Yarmouth was planning to change its name in his honour to *The Nelson Arms* and, though certainly pleased, joked that it was inappropriate as he had only the one arm. Someone in Tenerife, which is also proud of its association with Nelson, remembered that story when implementing a similar plan. At Puerto de la Cruz, 18 miles south of Santa Cruz, there is a bar called *Nelson's Arm*. Obviously someone took on board Nelson's observation! Postcards of pubs named after Nelson could form a very different sort of Nelson collection, I suppose.

In choosing postcards for this section, my aim has been to draw attention to, rather than to define, the variety. A comprehensive coverage is impossible and certainly cannot be achieved in a book restricted to 200 illustrations.

Nelson was so popular that he was asked to give his name to a variety of things while alive. On his holiday tour in 1802, for example, the *Morning Star* newspaper declared that there was *"no man so busily employed in England"* after he was invited to name hostelries as well as prize farm animals and produce. Since then, his name has been used as a brand name on many products. Popular in his own time, he has, during the last 200 years, helped to promote a wide variety of products. Associated names such as *Trafalgar* and *Victory* extend that range even further.

Postcards which feature *Nelson* and associated names such as *Trafalgar* as brand names are hard for the collector to find but would make an interesting collection. Postcards from the 'Golden Age' featuring items that belonged to or were used by Nelson are more difficult to find. It seems scenes from Nelson's life, reproduced on postcards, gripped the postcard collector of yesterday rather than did the postcards showing 'real' Nelson material - Nelson's everyday belongings, his clothes and his furniture. Demand led the market and there were significantly more of the former type of postcard produced. The collector need not be completely deprived, though, as museums today are filling the gap by publishing modern colour photographic postcards such as the one included here of Lord Nelson's Medicine Chest.

Nelson's legacy was diverse and even resulted in some new phrases in the English language. Best known is 'to turn a blind eye' which is often said to have been inspired by Nelson's behaviour at the Battle of Copenhagen. Well known among the cricket fraternity is the 'Nelson' or 'Lord Nelson', a score of 111 which, as a consequence of superstitious belief, results in cricketers and occasionally umpires lifting a foot off the ground when a score of 111 is on the scoreboard. The whole ritual is mistakenly founded on the belief that Nelson had one eye, one arm and one leg (though the recently-retired cricket umpire David Shepherd, who hops on one leg when the score reaches 111 or a multiple thereof, claims it was one eye, one arm, and one sugar in a cup of tea!).

Less well-known is the phrase 'to tap the admiral', which appeared in Royal Navy language in the latter part of the nineteenth century, meaning to enjoy strong alcoholic drink. This is based on a story that sailors, desperate for drink, bored a hole in the cask of brandy in which Nelson's body was being transported home, so that they could enjoy a tipple. The story also claimed that the cask was empty on arrival home. Nelson is also, apparently, the origin of the phrase 'to push the boat out'. Nelson had Madeira or Claret in decanters on his dining table. He had a silver-wheeled boat on the table to hold the decanters and would push the wine around the table to his guests. His boat has survived in the Lloyds Nelson Collection.

Whether or not there are postcards that in any way illustrate these expressions is something I cannot answer, except in the case of the first phrase. One card is included in this book in the section on Nelson's life. The locating of others is another Nelson collecting challenge.

Nelson's undress uniform coat, worn on the day of the Battle of Trafalgar, along with the other clothes he wore on that fateful day, is kept at the National Maritime Museum at Greenwich. It is easy to see how well his insignia would have made him stand out. This postcard clearly shows that the Gold Star of The Turkish Order of the Crescent was sewn on the wrong way round.

The damaged and displaced epaulette on the left shoulder of the coat, and a hole in the coat itself indicate the place where the fatal musket ball entered Nelson's body. Remnants of the epaulette, coat and shirt were found with the ball when it was removed from the body during the autopsy. The surgeon, Dr Beatty, wore a locket containing the ball and fabric fragments which he bequeathed to Queen Victoria and the Royal Collection. Captain Hardy gave Nelson's coat and waistcoat to Emma Hamilton, though ownership resided with the new Earl Nelson, who allowed her to keep the coat on loan. After Emma fled to France in debt, the coat and waistcoat reappeared in 1845 in the ownership of the widow of JJ Smith, a former City alderman, who wanted £150 for them. The Prince Consort, Albert, bought them and presented them to Greenwich Hospital.

Nelson had several coats, and a number of these are preserved. Personal items of Admiral Nelson were kept on board HMS *Nelson* until the outbreak of World War II. A Trafalgar uniform coat normally kept on board was sent ashore to the National Bank of Scotland in Thurso for safe keeping, but a lock of his hair was retained as a good luck charm.

140. Nelson's Trafalgar Uniform, National Maritime Museum - published by Pitkin Pictorials Ltd.

Many of Nelson's other personal effects were kept, and there was clearly an awareness at the time of his death that it was a moment of great significance and therefore important that everything possible should be treasured and safeguarded.

As has already been said, early postcards of Nelson's belongings such as this example are scarce. This one shows Nelson's fighting sword, a portion of the Union Flag (incorporated in the White Ensign) flown at Trafalgar, his hat, his ice pails and an example of a combined knife and fork. Nelson, after the loss of his right arm, had several of these and found them useful. The items shown here were preserved in the Royal United Services Museum that used to be in Whitehall. Items were later sold, and a fragment of the Union Jack was one item sold into private ownership.

A Trafalgar veteran, Frank Jenkins, sold his nine-inch fragment of flag in 1904 for £650. More recently, on 28 September 2004, Bonham's auction house sold a piece of flag, claimed at the funeral by J Constable, with an 1856 letter of provenance for £47,800 - little more than the 1904 value when inflation-adjusted!

ROYAL UNITED SERVICE MUSEUM.   WHITEHALL.
1. Lord Nelson's Fighting Sword.
2. A portion of the Union Flag flown on board the "Victory" during the battle.
3. Lord Nelson's Gold Combined Knife and Fork for one hand.
4. Lord Nelson's Cocked Hat.   5. Lord Nelson's Ice-pails.

141. Royal United Service Museum Whitehall - published by Gale & Polden Kelkel Series

The centrepiece of this equally scarce postcard is a lower portion of one of *Victory*'s Trafalgar masts. It had a horse-shoe at the base, nailed there as a lucky charm by Nelson's crew. A French cannonball made the hole in the mast. Though it is described here as the main mast, it is thought to be a part of the foremast. It was at one time used as a pedestal for a Nelson bust that was commissioned from Chantrey in 1833 by the Duke of Clarence.

Later, as William IV, he kept it in a garden temple at Bushey Lodge, where robins nested in it. It was moved to Windsor Castle and eventually donated to the Royal United Services Museum by King Edward VII, together with the other items in the picture - sections of the jib boom and the mizzen top mast which was shot in two early in the battle. The double-headed bar shot, which killed 8 marines in *Victory*, was fired from the Spanish *Santissima Trinidad,* while the single shot which can be seen near the mast section was from *Victory*'s shot locker.

ROYAL UNITED SERVICE MUSEUM. WHITEHALL.
1. Portions of the "Victory's" Mainmast, Jib-boom and Mizzen-topmast.
2. Chantrey's Bust of Lord Nelson. 3. Lord Nelson's Wash-stand.
4. Double-headed Shot fired from the Spanish Flagship into the "Victory," killing 8 of her crew.

143. Lord Nelson's Inkstand - published by Raphael Tuck & Sons Ltd Real Photograph Series no. 5178

An Interesting Souvenir. LORD NELSON'S INKSTAND.
ON BOARD THE "VICTORY" AT THE BATTLE OF TRAFALGAR OCTOBER 21st, 1805.

Another of the postcards showing Nelson memorabilia is this card of an inkstand which was in Nelson's cabin on *Victory*. Before the Battle of Trafalgar, Nelson would have used this to write the codicil to his will and also his famous prayer. Nelson memorabilia can be found in both public and private collections and pieces still appear at auction. Great care is needed in assessing provenance as many fake pieces have been manufactured and other genuine pieces copied.

144. Lord Nelson's Medicine Chest - published by Burnham Thorpe PCC

It was common for naval officers to carry their own supply of medicines, and chests such as the one shown on this modern postcard could conveniently carry bottles, pills, powders and lotions as well as a balance for weighing drugs. Pincers, scissors, drug recipes and so on would also be included. There was, of course, a surgeon (doctor) on *Victory* as well with his own remedies and instruments.

This medicine chest, which belonged to Nelson, is now the property of All Saints Church in Burnham Thorpe, which also has a gift to Nelson by the City of Norwich following the 1798 Battle of the Nile. This is an engraved glass goblet bearing the words *"ADMIRAL NELSON GLORIOUS"*.

145. Nelson Collection, Monmouth - published by Raphael Tuck & Sons Ltd 'Real Photograph' Postcard

The Nelson Museum at Monmouth, a section of which is featured on this postcard, houses a large collection of Nelson memorabilia, including pictures, letters, silver, china and Nelson's only known fighting sword and telescope. It is also home to the Lady Nelson papers. A lot of the material was bequeathed to the town of Monmouth by Lady Llangattock, mother of Charles Rolls of Rolls Royce fame. Her bequest, which included both genuine and fake items, was added to the collection already in the Museum.

146. Bucklers Hard. Where The Agamemnon Was Built - publisher unknown

Many places in Britain are proud of some link to Nelson, including Buckler's Hard close to Beaulieu in Hampshire. Buckler's Hard (originally Buckle's Hard) developed from 1743 as a shipbuilding community with an output of mainly warships, but also some merchant vessels too. One of the latter was actually named *Nelson*. The evidence of the old slipways, such as the one pictured on this real photographic postcard, can still be seen by visitors today. Elsewhere in the book you will find a postcard showing a model of the village in the days when shipbuilding was a thriving industry. Now it is home to the very interesting Buckler's Hard Maritime Museum. Included in its fine displays are Nelson exhibits that include some of his baby clothes.

The Master Shipbuilder at Buckler's Hard was Henry Adams. He and his sons built many fine vessels, including three of the ships that fought at Trafalgar. These were *Agamemnon*, a 64 gun ship, *Euryalus*, of 36 guns and *Swiftsure*, with 74 guns. *Agamemnon* is believed to have been Nelson's favourite ship and she witnessed significant events in his life. He met Lady Hamilton in Naples and, later, lost the sight of his right eye at the siege of Calvi while serving as her captain.

147. Antigua's Memento of Horatio Nelson - published by The Friends of English Harbour, Antigua, W.I.

There are many places abroad associated with Nelson as he travelled extensively in his career. Antigua has always been proud of its links with Nelson and this composite postcard shows some sites that would have been familiar to him - though he was never there with HMS *Victory* which is featured on this postcard.

Postcards of sites with links to Nelson's service abroad would make an interesting collection. He saw service in many areas of the world including the West Indies, South America, the Arctic, the East Indies and, of course, Europe.

Interior of St John's Church, Figtree, Nevis, W.I. (Where the Register of Marriage of Lord Nelson is kept)

148. *Interior of St John's Church, Figtree, Nevis, W.I. (Where the Register of Marriage of Lord Nelson is kept) - published by A. Moure Losada, Basseterre, St Kitts No88a*

The marriage certificate of Horatio Nelson and Frances Nisbet is preserved here in St John's Church, Figtree, on the island of Nevis where they were married - as noted on one of several cards by this St Kitts publisher.

Apart from the Nevis postcards, other collectable postcards that recorded Nelson's life were published in Antigua by Jose Anjo. Publishers of postcards showing the Nelson Statue in Barbados include Roberts, Knight, Plimmer, Leder and Siefert.

This postcard shows another of the places in the West Indies that Nelson knew as a young man. The scene is a battery, sometimes called Fort Charles Battery, in Port Royal, Kingston, Jamaica. Nelson was in charge of the battery when fighting the French in 1779. The wooden deck of the upper tier of the battery is still called 'Nelson's Quarterdeck'.

The plaque on the wall reads: '*IN THIS PLACE DWELT HORATIO NELSON. You, who tread his footprints, remember his glory*'.

Nelson's Memorial Tablet, Jamaica, British West Indies.—25242.

149. *Nelson's Memorial Tablet, Jamaica, British West Indies - publisher unknown no. 25242*

150. *Anchor of the* Victory, *Nelson's flagship - published by Jarrold & Sons Ltd,* Jarrolds' *Series no. 2181*

In the introduction to this chapter, the variety of forms of memorial to Nelson was outlined. Southsea was particularly significant in the Nelson story and it is appropriate that the memorial there is a little different - an anchor from HMS *Victory*.

Postcards of HMS *Victory*'s anchor at Southsea can be found easily. Most postcard publishers have produced their versions and many are from the same viewpoint as the card pictured here. Nelson's last hours in England are well-documented, particularly his last walk down to the beach at Southsea where he boarded his barge to go out and join his ship. The monument, which features a genuine anchor from *Victory*, is close to the actual place from which Nelson left England for Trafalgar.

Nelson in Lancashire is one of the many places that have been named after Horatio Nelson. Former farming settlements in the Chapelry of Colne, Great Marsden and the area of Little Marsden around the Church of St Paul were renamed in honour of the national hero. A local inn in the centre of the town was named *Lord Nelson* in 1805, not long after the death of Nelson, and it is thought by some that the idea for the town's name came from there.

The coat of arms shown on this postcard reflects the nature of industry in the town - that of textiles. Two reed hooks are shown in the centre of the arms with a lamb and two cotton plants.

151. *Nelson - published by Stoddart & Co.,* Heraldic *Series*

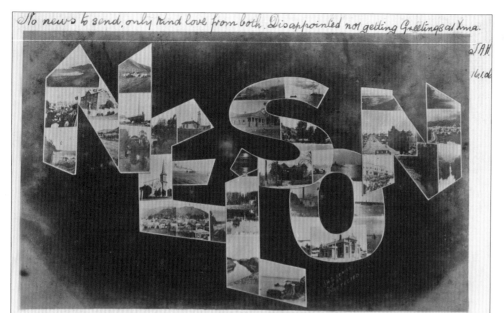

No news to send, only kind love from both. Disappointed not getting Greetings at Xmas.

152. Nelson - published by JHS, New Zealand

As has already been mentioned, Britain was not alone in honouring Nelson by naming towns, streets and mountains after him. This postcard, published in October 1905 in New Zealand to coincide with the Trafalgar Centenary, uses parts of 38 photographs of Nelson in New Zealand to spell out the famous hero's name.

The cathedral in Nelson in New Zealand is approached from Trafalgar Street. It seems to be often the case that even if the town or city was not named after Nelson or his victories then a number of features in a given town were - Trafalgar Street off Nelson Square or something along the same lines. The collector interested in such features will find a very large selection.

Other collectors gather postcards which feature large-lettered names, either of people or places. An example of the former can be found at the beginning of the next part of the book. I haven't come across any additional examples using Nelson's name, but I am sure there must be others.

153. 'Lord Nelson' (Southern) - published by R.S. (Ruskin Studio) Art Press Ltd

The Southern Railway named this 4-6-0 Express locomotive after the great man when it was built in 1926. It ran from Victoria to Folkestone and Dover. The reverse of the postcard tells us that *"on this route, schedule time being essential, only engines of the highest mechanical efficiency can be utilized"*. Other engines in the class were to be named after other 'names famous in the fighting history of England'.

154. *Model Yacht Pond In Nelson Gardens, Great Yarmouth - publisher unknown, card no. 4*

Nelson would probably have approved of this scene. In gardens named after him at one of his favourite places, Great Yarmouth, children and young-at-heart adults enjoy boating on the Model Yacht Pond in the 1920s.

155. *Battle of Trafalgar - publisher unknown*

Companies also used Nelson in postcard advertising material and in a variety of other ways. Some companies such as Shell and Price's Candles issued postcard-sized cards that had information on the side usually reserved for the message. They could not, of course, be postally used. Cassell's gave free postcards away to advertise their *Saturday Journal* and others followed suit. J & J Coleman of Norwich and London put free postcards in their boxes of starch - a precursor of the free items in cereal packets or given away at McDonald's. Some firms, for example McLintoch, pre-printed order forms on the message side of pictorial postcards such as their card of Lady Hamilton.

On this postcard, Pearks Tea sought to promote not just its tea but its butter, too: *"With every palate they agree, Pearks butter, Pearks tea"*. The reverse of the postcard tells us Pearks butter: *"Tastes like Cream"*.

Quite what the connection was with Nelson or his death at Trafalgar I am not sure!

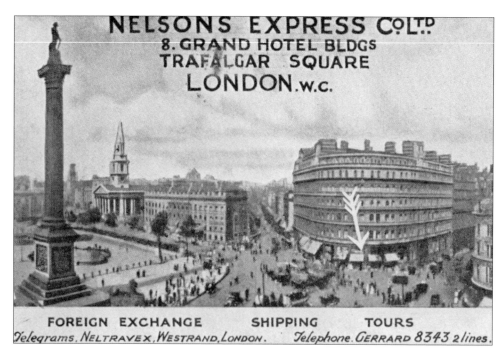

Many businesses across the world have traded, and still do trade, under a Nelson name. This postcard, which shows the Nelson Express Company's office in Trafalgar Square, was sent in 1927 by the company to tell a customer that a coach for Sheerness was fully booked. The company has cleverly sought to exploit its name link with the great man by the juxtaposition on the postcard of the picture of its office position with that of Nelson's Column. One wonders whether the office site was deliberately chosen with that possibility in mind or whether it was an opportunity seized.

No doubt there are many other examples of postcard advertising relying on association with the name, deeds and legacy of Nelson and thus the opportunity for building a very interesting postcard collection on that theme, too.

157. *HMS Nelson - publisher unknown*

Nelson would, I am sure, have been flattered had he known that large ships of the Royal Navy, in particular, would be named after him and his battles. Not long after his death, the first of a series of large warships was named after him. It was a three-decker of 120 guns laid down in 1809.

This scarce postcard is of the second ship in the series, the second HMS *Nelson*. She was an armoured cruiser, classed at that time as an armoured frigate. Launched in 1876, she spent a lot of time in the Pacific where her great operational range was particularly useful. She was of a transitional design, being barque-rigged for sail but also equipped with steam engines.

158. *HMS* Nelson - *published by Gale & Polden Ltd*

HMS *Nelson* was paid off in 1901 and moored at Portsmouth, where she became a Stokers Training Establishment before being sold to Dutch ship breakers in 1910. This real photographic postcard was taken late in her life - postally used, it is dated 1909.

The stern of the ship is a reminder of a previous generation and still echoes the design features with which Nelson himself would have been familiar. In the twentieth century the design of ships would change dramatically.

159. *Many Happy Returns From HMS* Lord Nelson - *publisher unknown, no. 21*

HMS *Lord Nelson* and her sister ship HMS *Agamemnon* were deliberately given their particular names in the hope that the Nelson link would inspire the Royal Navy at a time when Britain's naval supremacy was under threat for the first time since Trafalgar. They were designed with strong turreted secondary armour to combat destroyers and torpedo boats, and were considered to look un-English with their tripod masts, odd-sized funnels and high superstructure. Events, in any case, outdated both *Lord Nelson* and her sister before they were completed and they were almost immediately consigned to second-class status by the launching of the new Dreadnought class. *Lord Nelson* was paid off and sold for scrap in 1920.

The association of the ship HMS *Lord Nelson* with the man, Horatio Lord Nelson, is particularly emphasised on postcards such as this birthday greetings card.

Postcards of the more modern 'Nelson' ships, HMS *Lord Nelson* and the third and last (to date) HMS *Nelson* are easier to find. Most marine specialist postcard publishers produced examples. Many major publishers, local and national, used them as subjects and there are many pictures of them that cannot be attributed accurately. Postcards of *Lord Nelson* are usually pictures of her launch or views of the exterior of the ship. The comparison with these and the way in which the next HMS *Nelson* battleship was portrayed on postcards is interesting. Postcards of *Lord Nelson* reflect the times. They are exterior views and formal, apart from the occasional Birthday and Christmas cards, and make an interesting comparison with, for example, Stephen Cribb's cards of the last HMS *Nelson*.

This postcard shows a painting of the last major battleship to date to bear the Nelson name. HMS *Nelson* was laid down in 1923 and commissioned in 1927 and, with her sister ship HMS *Rodney*, was of quite distinctive design. This postcard is the original produced from a

160. HMS Nelson - *published by J Salmon Ltd no. 4756*

painting by Bernard WT Church . It was later re-issued at the time of the Second World War with details of the ship on the bottom front and a message from Winston Churchill on the back. A third post-war reprint was also issued - of poorer quality but still with information about the ship on the front.

HMS *Nelson* became flagship to the Home Fleet on Trafalgar Day, 1927. She served with distinction in many of the major operations of the Second World War but ended her life ignominiously, being used as a bombing target in the Firth of Forth until being scrapped in 1950.

HMS *Nelson's* home port was Portsmouth and she features at anchor there on other postcards. She was a popular postcard subject, being photographed from the air and in other parts of the world such as Malta and the Panama Canal. A number of postcards can be collected showing her firing her broadside. The one-ton shells fired from her 16-inch guns could travel up to twenty miles.

Stephen Cribb, a Southsea photographer, took many wonderful pictures that were later published on postcards. His HMS *Nelson* series is particularly noteworthy and seems to have been published shortly after the ship was commissioned in 1927. This card shows HMS *Victory* as seen from HMS *Nelson*. It is from a fine set of about 30 postcards by the

161. HMS Nelson, *Passing Lord Nelson's Flagship* Victory - *published by Stephen Cribb, Southsea*

Southsea photographer. Cribb's series not only shows external features of the ship but also crew and officer spaces inside, with men at work or rest. These postcards of HMS *Nelson* are evidence of early attempts to put a human face on the serious subjects of war and weapons.

The single pictures and sets by Stephen Cribb or Wright & Logan were probably sold on board and would naturally have been a popular buy for the crew to send home. Many of these cards are found without evidence of posting, and some of my collection are probably typical in having been sent through the post in an envelope.

HMS *Nelson*, pre-Second World War, carried one of Horatio Nelson's Trafalgar uniforms, as well as other personal items. A lock of Nelson's hair was retained as a valued charm when the other items were placed for safe keeping in the National Bank of Scotland at Thurso, on the outbreak of war. This and other Nelson mementoes, such as a copy of the *Times* report of the Battle of the Nile, were still displayed in the ship until she was paid off in 1947.

The picture emphasises the pride HMS *Nelson* always had in her association with Nelson, *Victory* and the Trafalgar tradition.

162. Ship's Crest From HMS Nelson *Burnham Thorpe Church - published by Gilbert White, no. GW8*

SHIPS CREST FROM H.M.S. NELSON
BURNHAM THORPE CHURCH

G W 8   COPYRIGHT GILBERT WHITE

The crest of HMS *Nelson* is featured on this postcard. It was presented to All Saints Church at Burnham Thorpe on Trafalgar Day 1955, the 150th anniversary of the battle. The church also has flags from the ship.

The crest is on a white field with a lion rampant holding a palm branch in his paw. The lion rampant can be seen to be part of Horatio Nelson's coat-of-arms. The motto of the ship was also that of Horatio Nelson - Palmam Qui Meruit Ferat.

Stephen Cribb. Southsea.

SILVER BELL PRESENTED TO H.M.S. "NELSON" BY THE INHABITANTS OF NEWCASTLE-UPON-TYNE. 15th. SEPT. 1928.   WEIGHT 2.000 OZS.

HMS *Nelson* was built on the River Tyne at Walker's Naval Yard, and the inhabitants of Tyneside presented the ship with a silver bell on 15th September 1928. Here the bell is pictured on a Stephen Cribb postcard. The bell was returned to Newcastle-upon-Tyne Council when the ship was scrapped. In 1974 the city gave it to HMS *Nelson* Barracks at Portsmouth.

163. Silver Bell Presented To HMS Nelson *By The Inhabitants Of Newcastle-upon-Tyne 15th Sept 1928 - published by Stephen Cribb, Southsea*

164. Untitled - Three members of the Nelson Battalion, Royal Naval Division - publisher unknown

Sailors or soldiers? Nelson would probably have been confused, too. At the outbreak of the First World War, the Reserves of the Royal Navy numbered some 20-30,000 men. There were insufficient places for them on Royal Navy ships and it was decided to form them into the 63rd (Royal Naval) Division. These men belonged to the *Nelson* Battalion. Fighting originally in Belgium, the Royal Naval Division went on to fight in the Gallipoli Campaign, where it suffered very heavy casualties, and then in Western Europe until the end of the war, by which time almost 48,000 men had been killed. As men were lost, recruits were advertised for - *"Handymen to fight on Land and Sea"*. They had to be between 18 and 38 years old, with a minimum chest measurement of 34 inches and minimum height of five feet three and a half inches. Pay was one shilling and three pence per day with Family Allowances.

Royal Naval Division, *Nelson* Battalion, postcards are hard to find. This rare postcard has the names of the men on the back and a note that they were the *"Gallant Three"* of the 11th Platoon - *"Boys in Khaki, Boys in Blue"*.

WRECK OF THE FOUDROYANT.

A notable event in local lifeboat service occurred on the 16th June, 1897, when the Blackpool Lifeboat put out to Nelson's old Flagship, the "Foudroyant," which was wrecked a little to the north of the North Pier. This fine old battleship had been brought to Blackpool on exhibition, but in a sudden gale her cables snapped, and she was driven aground and became a total wreck. On this occasion the crew of 28 were all saved. The record of the Blackpool Lifeboat Service is a grand total of over 136 lives.
[From a photo taken at the time.]

165. Wreck of the Foudroyant *- published by the Royal National Lifeboat Institution, Blackpool Branch*

Foudroyant, a former flagship of Nelson, remained on station and in active service until 1862, when she was re-employed as a gunnery training ship. Her service life over, there were proposals to sell her 30 years later for scrap. However, her association with Nelson was not forgotten and by public demand she was saved from being broken up when she was bought as a boys training ship by Mr Wheatley Cobb, who restored her to a state that allowed her to be sailed. She was on a fund-raising propaganda cruise around Britain when she was wrecked on Blackpool Sands on 16 June 1897.

With no hope of salvage and restoration, the wreck was eventually broken up and many items were produced from her wood and copper.

Most postcards offered for sale today show Nelson's *Foudroyant* as a wreck on Blackpool beach. The two shown in this chapter are among the more difficult to find.

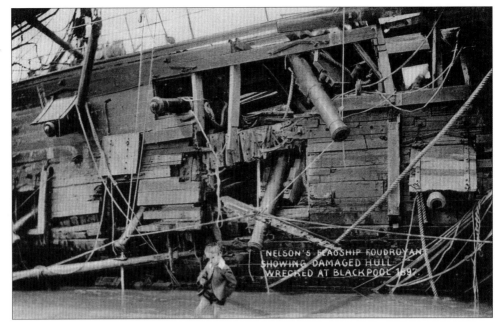

166. Nelson's Flagship Foudroyant Showing damaged Hull, Wrecked at Blackpool 1897 - published by Misch & Co. Nelson Centenary Series 317/12

Much of the wood from the wreck of *Foudroyant* went to be made into furniture. Waring and Gillow, the London furniture makers, held an exhibition of items made from *Foudroyant* timber in October 1905. Many pieces were copies of furniture used by Nelson himself. The wood panelling of Blackpool Football Club's Boardroom was *Foudroyant* oak. Some pieces of the ship simply became souvenirs, as they were just taken away by visitors to the wreck.

Much of the copper went to the Birmingham Mint that made approximately 25,000 medals between 1897 and the Trafalgar Centenary in 1905. The earliest medals show a picture of *Foudroyant* and identify the copper as having come from the ship. The Nelson Centenary medal struck for the British and Foreign Sailors' Society in 1905 shows Nelson and *Victory*. Another medal issue was made in 1955 for the 150th anniversary of Trafalgar.

167. Implacable (formerly Duguay Trouin) - published by Opie Ltd no. 534

This real photographic postcard shows another ship associated with Nelson and Trafalgar in particular - HMS *Implacable*. As *Duguay Trouin*, she was a survivor of the Trafalgar Franco-Spanish fleet, only to be captured after the battle. Fifth in line in the combined enemy fleet, she was isolated by Nelson's line-cutting and only got back to the main action at about 3.15pm by which time the battle was as good as won. She escaped with fourteen other ships but was eventually captured on 4 November by Admiral Richard Strachan. Re-named HMS *Implacable*, she saw service in the Royal Navy and spent time later in her life moored in sight of HMS *Victory*.

After the destruction of the original *Foudroyant* Mr Wheatley Cobb bought HMS *Trincomalee* and re-named her *Foudroyant*. After Wheatley Cobb's death, *Foudroyant* eventually joined HMS *Implacable* in 1932 to form a youth training establishment run by the Foudroyant Trust.

Implacable's condition eventually became a serious concern. She was paid off in 1947 and because her repair needs were considered too costly, she was towed into the English Channel and, on 2 December 1949, sunk.

Part Three
Nelson: The Memory

Chapter Six
Trafalgar Day, Centenary, Special Times

The anniversary of Nelson's great victory and death, Nelson's special day, 21 October, has been commemorated at least since 1824 when the custom of holding a Trafalgar Anniversary Dinner on board HMS *Victory* began.

The custom of honouring Nelson on that day spread, and many towns and villages began to arrange special Trafalgar Day Services in thanksgiving. The prime mover behind the promotion of Trafalgar Day was the Navy League, whose immediate motives, while patriotic and appreciative of Nelson, were to champion the preservation of a strong navy. In 1895 they introduced to the capital the Trafalgar Day celebration in Trafalgar Square. National enthusiasm increased, and the custom became a national event.

21st October 1905 marked the hundredth anniversary of the battle, and while there was recognition that the Anglo-French *Entente Cordiale* meant that jingoistic celebration would be inappropriate, it was also noted that the Centenary festivities would do recruiting for an undermanned navy no harm. A major celebration was arranged by the Navy League in Trafalgar Square in London to mark the occasion, and in cities, towns and villages the nation's people held their own tree plantings and thanksgiving services. Similar scenes of celebration of Nelson and his achievements took place around the world.

Postcard publishers, seeing a commercial opportunity, produced large numbers of postcards featuring Nelson and, in so doing, both responded to a national mood and fuelled it. General interest in Nelson reached new heights. The postcard marketing competition was joined by all the major publishers, as well as by many provincial challengers. The result was a rich variety of Nelson cards.

The great majority of examples of Nelson postcards found today date from this centenary period and significant among these are the various special anniversary cards. Some are featured here. They vary in value and a glance through the stock of one or two dealers will explain why. One or two can be found easily but others are scarce. In collecting postcards of local centenary celebrations, the Nelson collector is in competition with the topographical collector, particularly with regard to real photographic locally-published cards. These can command high prices.

At the time of writing, surprisingly few bicentenary postcards have appeared. The Isle of Wight (UK) Postcard Club has, though, issued a limited edition card, which is a welcome publication, and so have J Salmon of Sevenoaks and Pageantry Postcards. These are welcome publications, which hopefully will be joined soon by a number of others.

168. 1805 Souvenir 1905 NELSON - published by Rotary Photographic Co. Ltd no. 5157A

The year 1905, one hundred years after the Battle of Trafalgar, signalled a huge increase in the number and types of Nelson-linked postcards, but this was only a part of a massive interest at the time in postcards generally. Postcard quality benefited as publishers themselves battled for their share of the market, and some of the postcards that resulted were outstanding in design and production.

The fine example shown here employs vignettes to summarise the life and achievements of Nelson. Other postcards captured the flavour of local celebrations and were obviously published with a view to maximising local sales. Such postcards tend to be scarce as they are also of interest to collectors of local history in those areas.

Celebration of Trafalgar Day began about 40 years after the Battle of Trafalgar. Garlands of laurel were placed on HMS *Victory* at the spot where Nelson fell and also on the mastheads. John Pasco, who, as Nelson's Flag Lieutenant, was in charge of hoisting the famous signal, instituted the Trafalgar Dinner ceremony in 1846. Pasco, who later became Captain of *Victory*, began the Trafalgar Dinner ceremony but did not initiate the flying of the famous signal on the ship each year on 21 October. That practice began later in the century.

In 1895, the Navy League began the tradition of holding a Trafalgar Day Service in Trafalgar Square. It took upon itself the role of Column decorator, hanging garlands from the jaws of the lions and the Column each Trafalgar Day, for many years. The Navy League was a pressure group supporting and promoting the role of the Navy. Postcards from the period show the practice of draping laurel and flags on the column and lions. The Navy League printed a special message on the reverse of a postcard commissioned from Raphael Tuck: *"The Executive Committee of the Navy League respectively ask for a continuance of your generous patronage and practical support. As requested I venture to remind you that your subscription of One Shilling fell due on the 1st...... PJ Hannon Secretary 11, Victoria Street, London SW"*. Various versions of Navy League message cards can be found.

169. The Nelson Column, Trafalgar Square. Decorated By The Navy League On Trafalgar Day (Oct 21st) - published by Raphael Tuck & Sons Ltd for The Navy League

170. England expects that every man this day will do his duty - published by S.M. Gibson & Co.

This is one of the four bas-reliefs at the base of Nelson's Column in Trafalgar Square. The reliefs depict Nelson's battles. One, by ML Watson, is of Nelson after the Battle of St Vincent, accepting the surrender of swords from the defeated Spanish Captains. Others, by WF Woodington and J Ternough respectively, show the victories of the Nile and Copenhagen.

The scene on this postcard, sculpted by JE Carew, 'Death of Nelson at Trafalgar', shows the wounded Nelson being taken from HMS *Victory*'s deck after being shot by the marksman on *Redoutable*. The reliefs were made from the bronze of captured cannon. The Navy League decorations indicate that the photograph for the postcard picture was probably taken in centenary year, 1905.

These celebrations attracted large patriotic crowds and were repeated in other parts of the country. For the centenary of the Battle of Trafalgar in 1905, the decoration of Nelson's Column by the Navy League went even further, with Nelson's Trafalgar signal and a rope of laurel dressing the column from top to bottom. A huge Union Jack flew from the pedestal. As can be seen on this postcard view, the crowd celebrating in the square was enormous. It was reported that the Trafalgar Square Centenary celebration drew a crowd of approximately a million people!

171. London. Nelson's Column, Trafalgar Square, Oct 21st 1905. Centenary Battle of Trafalgar - published by J Valentine & Co.

London. Nelson's Column, Trafalgar Square, Oct. 21, 1905. Centenary Battle of Trafalgar

Nelson's Statue 21st Oct. 1905, Barbados

In Barbados, the London scene was echoed. The Nelson Statue in Trafalgar Square, Barbados, was similarly decorated. Though there was considerable interest, the postcard shows those making up the crowd as a little more restrained than their London counterparts.

NELSON CENTENARY CELEBRATIONS

This real photographic card shows a small section of the scene of celebration around the statue in the Liverpool Mansion House quadrangle. A huge wreath of laurel is draped around the statue and a smaller wreath at the top. Bunting, flags and ribbons would have made it a colourful scene. Unfortunately, as this is a monochrome postcard, we are unable to appreciate that fully.

173. Nelson Centenary Celebrations - published by T Roth

HMS *Victory*, the largest single relic associated with Nelson, commands a special place in any celebration of Nelson's life and of Trafalgar, though that has not always been the case, and she could easily have been lost to us through neglect.

The majority of postcards that show *Victory* decorated with laurel garlands and flying the Trafalgar signal date from the Centenary year of 1905 but it is not always easy to tell at a glance. Although postal dates and messages on the backs are clues, it is helpful to have additional information. Publishers, trying to keep costs down, tended to re-use photographs if they could, so re-touching, tinting, re-titling and other techniques were not uncommon.

This postcard does show HMS *Victory* at the time of the Centenary. The submarine, B1, is shown alongside her. B1, which had been launched a year before, was providing power for the floodlighting of HMS *Victory* during the celebrations.

The decoration of HMS *Victory*, with Nelson's Trafalgar Signal and with laurel garlands, was introduced late in the nineteenth century by one of the Admiral's Superintendents of Portsmouth Dockyard. The signal was not seen in quite the same way as at Trafalgar when it would have been made using twelve hoists on the mizzen-mast alone. Now it was displayed using all three masts so that the whole signal could be flown at once.

Until 1908, the wrong codebook was used and the collector will find many postcards showing both the incorrect, and later, the correct flag sequence *(see also illus. 51 & 52)*. As has already been mentioned, a special service is still held on *Victory* and a special Nelson Dinner still held in Nelson's cabin each Trafalgar Day when the Immortal Memory toast is still drunk.

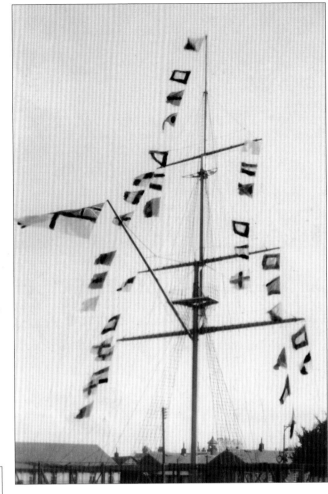

176. Untitled (Shotley Royal Naval Training Establishment) - published by Edith F Driver, Ipswich

This postcard shows the Trafalgar Day signal being flown at Shotley Royal Naval Training Establishment, near Ipswich. Shotley became the home of the HMS *Ganges* training establishment. The flags on this black and white photograph have been hand-coloured, a practice commonly known as tinting.

In 1895, the Navy League Trafalgar Square commemorative service was replicated, particularly in Naval establishments at home and abroad. A special service was also held in Penzance in Cornwall, where the news of the Battle of Trafalgar and Nelson's death arrived in November 1805.

NELSON CENTENARY 1905.

ENGLAND

S.GEORGE'S CROSS

UNITED KINGDOM

FIRST UNION JACK 1606 - 1800

DIAGRAM SHOWING THE

SALTIRES OF S.ANDREW & S.PATRICK COUNTERCHANGED

SCOTLAND

S.ANDREWS CROSS (SALTIRE)

IRELAND

S. PATRICKS CROSS (SALTIRE)

BRITISH EMPIRE

THE UNION JACK 1801 TO PRESENT DAY

The Red Cross of S. George, dating back from the days of the Crusades, is the old flag of England ; under it the gallant seamen of the Elizabethan era sailed, explored and fought, and saved the country from the threatened invasion by the Spanish Armada. When this Island became one Kingdom under James I., the Cross of S. George was united with the Cross of S. Andrew, Scotland's national flag, and thus was formed the first Union Jack. Except for a brief period during the Commonwealth, this was the flag of the United Kingdom until the end of 1800, and was the flag under which Nelson fought at S. Vincent (1797), and to which he added such lustre by his glorious and complete victory at the mouth of the Nile (1798).

On January 1st, 1801, the red saltire of S. Patrick was introduced into the flag, counterchanged with the saltire of S. Andrew, the broad white of the latter being uppermost next the staff. The field of the flag remained blue, and the whole was surmounted by the Cross of S. George with its white border, thus forming the national emblem which bears in its folds all the glories and traditions of our race.

It emerged successfully from its baptism of fire at Copenhagen (1801), and when at Trafalgar, Oct. 21st, 1805, our greatest Admiral gave his life for his country, his brilliant career and devotion to duty had, in his final victory, secured for Britain the sovereignty of the seas.

ENT'D. AT STATIONERS HALL.

This postcard is another of the many and varied offerings produced for the *Nelson Centenary 1905*, the event we know better as the Trafalgar Centenary. The postcard reminded Edwardians of the history and development of the Union Flag, still known as the Union Jack, and that, at the time of Trafalgar, the flag was only four years old.

177. Nelson Centenary 1905 - published by WS Cowell, Ipswich, the Christchurch Series

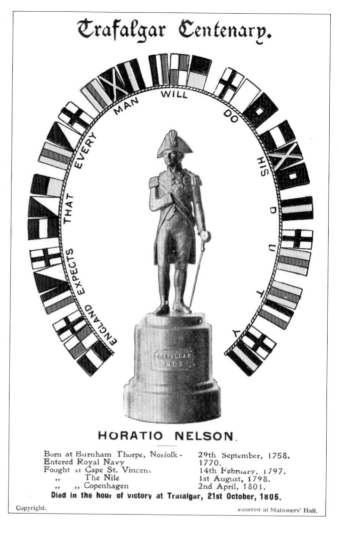

Postcard publishers exercised all their invention and skill to produce attractive, interesting cards to celebrate the Trafalgar Centenary. This one cleverly combines the statue of Nelson with the Trafalgar Signal and shows significant dates in Nelson's life. Typically, the flags depicted are the wrong ones. They are not from the codebook that would have been used at Trafalgar.

The postcard appears in at least one other variation, which has a different title. In place of the words *Nelson Centenary*, the alternative title is *County Borough of Great Yarmouth*. This second postcard shows the Great Yarmouth Borough Coat of Arms and the *Trafalgar Centenary* wording appears as *Nelson Centenary*, together with the date of the Battle of Trafalgar.

179. The Nelson Centenary 1805 - 1905. Celebrations At Great Yarmouth - published by AW Yallop, Great Yarmouth

This is one of the finest Nelson Centenary cards. It shows the Winter Gardens celebrations at Great Yarmouth on 20 October 1905, which involved 3,000 children. To the left and right of the central picture, the familiar themes of 'then and now', which were used by other postcard publishers of the time as well, can also be seen on this card. HMS *Victory* is portrayed on the left and a battleship of the 1905 period on the right, while the postcard is full of other naval imagery.

180. Nelson Centenary 1805 - 1905 Foes Once - Friends Now - published by CR Moody & Co., Ryde

This postcard publisher has chosen to couple recognition of the Trafalgar Centenary with the recent agreement of the time with the French, known as the *Entente Cordiale*. There was concern in political quarters as the celebratory mood built up with the approach of the Trafalgar Centenary, as it was felt by some that it was past history and should not be allowed to disturb our new friendly alliance with the French - an early appearance of the political correctness phenomenon, perhaps!

This postcard represents that point of view well, while still being celebratory. It was reminding the public that, although we had been enemies once, friendship had blossomed. In emphasising that the present mattered more than the past, and that peace was preferable to war, the publisher was adopting a less triumphal, more modern approach. It is ironic that, despite a long alliance, that same national relationship is still being questioned by some and is still under strain from time to time today, one hundred years later, and two hundred years after Trafalgar.

This postcard was clearly produced in very large numbers, probably in response to popular demand, as it can readily be found today in the boxes of postcard dealers.

It is predominantly black, which is unusual, the only colour being provided by the laurel wreath around the picture of Nelson. The Nelson vignette is taken from the Charles Lucy painting of 1853. The rest of the black background is relieved by a series of small Nelson and HMS *Victory*-related pictures, one of which is the Trafalgar Prayer.

181. The Nelson Centenary 1905 - published by Knight Brothers, Knight Series no. 1465

182. *1805 Nelson 1905 - published by WE Byers & Co.*

This postcard featuring HMS *Victory* and HMS *London* is not one of the best in terms of manufacturing and printing quality but it is, nevertheless, particularly interesting because of the added interest of the back. A scarce card, it carries on its reverse an invitation/advert for The Royal Naval Volunteer Reserve's Trafalgar Day Centenary Celebration to be held at '*the Dome on Saturday October 21st, at 8 o'clock*'.

I realised that in my collection I had postcards of *Victory* pictured with a variety of other more modern vessels - HMS *Dreadnought,* HMS *Australia,* submarine *B1,* HMS *Hannibal,* HMS *Bellerophon,* submarine *No.3,* HMS *Indomitable,* HMS *Iron Duke* and HMS *Nelson* all featured - and I wondered how many other naval vessels appeared on similar cards. Perhaps that could be the focus of a follow-up collection!

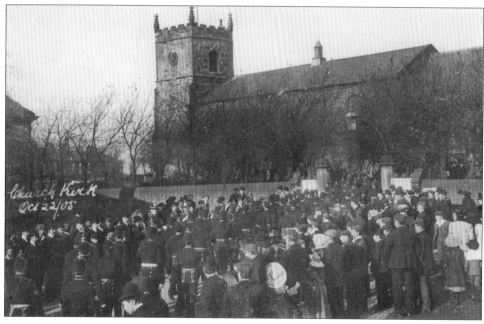

183. *Untitled (St James Church, Church Kirk, Lancashire - October 22nd 1905) - publisher unknown*

This is a real photographic postcard showing one of the many services held to celebrate the Trafalgar Centenary. It shows the crowd and Guard of Honour outside St James Church, Church Kirk, Lancashire, for the Centenary Service held there on 22 October 1905.

This type of local interest real photographic postcard is much sought-after by collectors of local history as well as by Nelson collectors.

A collection of postcards showing how the Trafalgar Centenary was celebrated in different parts of Great Britain and the world would make a very interesting collection!

184. *Nelson's dying words, 21st October 1805: "Thank God I have done my duty" - publisher unknown*

This postcard, like many Centenary postcards, used evocative imagery, in this case, a picture of Nelson together with the wording of the Trafalgar signal and Nelson's last words. The card, at first glance, appears rather plain, but on closer study can be seen to be a balanced, clever design - simple and effective.

185. *'England expects that every man will do his duty' 1805 2005 - published by the Isle of Wight UK Postcard Club Series 1 - no. 10*

This limited edition (of 2000) postcard has been produced by the Isle of Wight Postcard Club to mark the 2005 Bicentenary. According to the note on the back it is *"to commemorate Admiral Nelson aboard HMS Victory leading the English Fleet to victory at the 'Battle of Trafalgar' in 1805"*.

Chapter Seven
Inspiration and Example

Nelson's status as a national icon developed during the late Victorian period, fuelled by the confidence of a powerful nation. The best in everything was the national aspiration, and the great were captured in major works of art. Nelson's heroic death became first the inspiration for artists and, through their work replicated on postcards, an inspiration for the country. It was also largely during this period that the Nelson name spread to geographical features and buildings across the world. Nelson also became 'sanitised' and his human fallibilities either denied or re-interpreted. Today, Nelson and the details of his life are being re-examined and, with newly-discovered material and review of the old, our previous knowledge of Nelson is greater than ever before. He stands the test of time and still remains the embodiment of the true patriot.

The postcard examples in this section are illustrative of the variety of ways in which Nelson and past achievements were used in an attempt to inspire. The 1905 anniversary of Trafalgar and the upsurge of patriotism preceded the inexorable approach of conflict with Germany. There was still great faith placed in the Navy, championed by The Navy League from 1894, and Nelson was presented as an example to the Navy of what was expected.

On postcards of the time this sentiment can readily be seen. An official committee analysed the Battle of Trafalgar for any useful lessons and Nelson was projected as the outstanding example of initiative and patriotic bravery. In their own way, postcards, which were still very popular at the time, contributed in encouraging an almost fatal national self-belief. They were complicit in elevating expectation, particularly of the Navy and its leaders, that would prove impossible for them to satisfy. At the time, the supporters of a strong navy were delighted, as public opinion was a powerful influence in the debate on naval funding.

The admirals of the day are pictured on postcards beside Nelson and, in hope rather than fact, likened to him. In hindsight it is easy to see how hope became belief for many, and also how the reality of the strength of the German navy was able to catch the nation unawares.

The Navy League continued to work between the wars and kept the memory of Nelson alive with their decoration of the Nelson Column on Trafalgar Day, which it also designated a remembrance day for all sailors killed in the First World War.

"ENGLAND! WHAT THOU WERT, THOU ART!"
Henry Newbolt

186. 'England! What Thou Wert, Thou Art!' Henry Newbolt - published by Raphael Tuck & Sons Ltd. A Hundred Years Ago NELSON, no. 8719

Although I have chosen to use this postcard as an example of the manner in which Nelson was utilized as a patriotic icon, the postcard really links two of the Nelson themes in this book - Nelson's story as portrayed by artists and Nelson's importance as an inspirational figure.

Here, on a cleverly thought out Raphael Tuck postcard published at the time of the Trafalgar Centenary, (possibly inspired by Edward R Taylor's 1883 painting *Twas a famous victory*), this painting by Albert W Holden shows the modern sailor of the time gazing at a display of Nelson pictures. The line by Henry Newbolt directs us to interpret the scene in a particularly patriotic way.

Sir Henry John Newbolt (1862-1938) was an author and poet whose reputation was made by his ballads published in *Admirals All* in 1897. During the First World War, he was controller of wireless and cables but by that time he had published a succession of patriotic works including perhaps the best known, *Drake's Drum*. His reward was to be knighted in 1915.

Nelson proved to be good promotional material. His image had appeared at some time on almost every type of item manufactured, and he appeared on postcards increasingly when the country was faced with war.

This postcard associates Nelson, HMS *Victory* and Nelson's expectations with HMS *Dreadnought,* the symbol of the all-powerful Navy. The message is clear.

Note the inclusion, in the transcription of the message, of the words 'this day' - words Nelson did not use but which came from the song *The Death of Nelson*.

187. England expects that every man this day will do his duty - published by WW Russell & Co. The Modern Series

England expects that every man this day will do his duty

THE VICTORY.   THE DREADNOUGHT.

Lord Nelson

"THANK GOD, I HAVE
DONE MY DUTY"

The following lines were written by Nelson just before he left
Yarmouth for Copenhagen in 1801.

"I only now long to be gone, time is precious and
every hour makes more resistance. Strike quick and
home, and may we soon return victorious is the
fervent wish and shall be the hearty exertion of your
faithful and obliged   NELSON & BRONTE."

Let these immortal words become the " fervent
wish" and "hearty exertion' of every English-
man who is physically capable of answering his
country's call to arms. By doing this he will
show the world that the modern men of England
possess the character and courage worthy of her
ancient traditions.
                                GLADYS STOREY.

188. "Thank God I Have
Done My Duty" - published
by CW Faulkner & Co. Ltd

This postcard was published to raise money for the Gladys Storey Fund. Miss Gladys Storey OBE, supported by George V, established the fund during the Great War to pay for supplies of Bovril to be sent to soldiers in the trenches. The card is strong in its reminder of the Nelson legacy of fearless sacrifice for King and Country, using a sample of Nelson's handwriting, Union Flag and portrait to support Gladys' own exhortation.

Another card that at first glance looks the same is *Thank God I Have Done My Duty* published for the Gladys Storey Fund by Henry Good & Son, London. When the two cards are compared it can be seen that, although the general layout is the same, the flag is differently styled, the message is different, and the border is red rather than blue. Whereas there is a clear call to arms message on the card pictured here, the message on the red-bordered version, which seems to have been published later, is extolling the virtues of the British Empire.

Apparently versions of these cards also exist with the White Ensign in place of the Union Flag.

The Dreadnought imagery is used again on this striking post-card, and the message is brief and to the point - Nelson was unbeatable and HMS *Dreadnought* will be the same. The purpose of this card was to reassure and remind the purchaser of a proud heritage. It was cleverly designed, using over-laying of images. The result is that Nelson, as the designer intended, appears as a triumphant spirit of the past, keeping a safeguarding watch on the events of the time.

189. Dreadnoughts New &
Old - published J Salmon
Ltd

DREADNOUGHTS

NEW & OLD

190. *Three Cheers for the Red, White and Blue - publisher unknown, no. 485-1*

Three Cheers
for the
Red, White,
and Blue.

Related thinking lay behind this postcard with its combination of Admirals and Flagships - the old and the new (Admiral Jellicoe) - with the most important and largest symbol behind the smaller inserts on the card. To emphasise the Union Jack's importance, there is the Red, White and Blue message to reinforce the patriotic purpose.

Collectors will find a number of similar postcards on which Nelson and the Union Jack are the central images - Nelson in the foreground and the Union Jack in the background, yet dominating. The jury is out on whether the fact that the ships are showing their sterns is intended to convey an additional message!

ENGLAND·EXPECTS·THAT·EVERY
MAN·THIS·DAY·WILL·DO·HIS·DUTY.

But·yield·proud·
··foe,thy·fleet·
With·crews, at··
·∴·Britain's·feet·
And·make·submission·
·········meet·
To·our·King.·

BATTLE OF THE BALTIC.

On this attractively-designed postcard the central inset picture of Nelson, from the original painting by Abbott, is combined with flags and the Trafalgar Signal (wrong wording again!) together with decorated verse.

The extract is from verse five of Thomas Campbell's work *The Battle of the Baltic.* The intention, as in so many of the patriotic Nelson postcards, is to invoke or appeal to the patriotic pride of the would-be recruit through the combination of imagery, rousing words and reminders of past glory.

191. *England Expects That Every Man This Day will Do His Duty - published by Wildt & Kray, London, no. 3255*

192. *A Glorious Record And We Can Play it Over Again -* published by Inter-Art Co. *Comrade II Series, no. 970*

Using a pun on 'record' - record of Naval success and a gramophone record *Twas on Trafalgar Day* - this postcard uses a humorous approach to achieve the same morale-boosting ends. Fred Spurgin (1882-1968), who designed this card, was a well-known illustrator of the time and his post-cards are collected in their own right. He worked for several publishers, including Art & Humour Publishing Company, Avenue Publishing Company, EJ Hey & Co, Inter-Art Co, Thridgould & Co and Watking and Kracke.

Although this is only an illustration of a gramophone record, some postcards were produced with miniature, playable gramophone records attached, and these, too, are collectable.

Dominated by the large Union Jack, this two-colour card, once again juxtaposing the modern ship with HMS *Victory* is an affirmation of national intent. The wording of the Trafalgar signal is, this time, correct.

This card is postally used, and dated 3 September 1914. The card was obviously chosen by the sender for its caption as it summarised the writer's purpose, underlined in the written note.

"....we are not yet enlisted but expect to be by Thursday .... this is quite an experience, living with soldiers, but we will stick it. I think we will pass for certain".

193. *England Expects Every Man To Do His Duty -* published by Richardson & Co., Titchfield *Series no. 547*

Just in case civilians had not been persuaded to join up already, posters like this recruiting example from 1915, reproduced as a postcard, were aimed to encourage further recruiting to replace the lost men and fill the ranks. Its aim was to remind civilians of past glory and shame able-bodied men into rushing to sign up. Other efforts to encourage recruitment, such as Kitchener's famous *Your Country Needs You* poster, used similar patriotic, moral pressure, backed up by the order of the White Feather.

This shrewdly thought-out card can be appreciated at different levels. At one level it is simply a humorous card playing on the wording of Nelson's Trafalgar Signal. At another level it is illustrating the fond farewells familiar to thousands at the time of the beginning of the First World War. It is also a recruiting call, implying that, for men, the way to a woman's heart is to join up. Yet another interpretation of it escaped me, until I read the message on the back, written in 1916.

It appears to be from sister to brother: *"You must excuse this card, as I think it is a little on the naughty side"*. It is a reminder that social norms have changed and that open references to courting and embracing still raised an eyebrow in some quarters at the time of publication. The message finishes, sadly, *"...I saw the scouts go down to church this morning, and your place was vacant"*.

195. A Call To Arms! - published by Raphael Tuck & Sons Ltd, A Call to Arms Series III, no. 8775

This postcard recognised the great symbolic importance of Nelson to Britain in 1914 - a fact that was to be underlined 26 years later by Adolf Hitler. The Kaiser is portrayed mockingly, revealing his invasion plan, the primary target of which is the downfall of Nelson.

The suggestion that Germany believed that the Nelson spirit was enshrined in one statue was confirmed in the Second World War when Hitler, as part of the Operation Sealion plan for the invasion of England, declared in an SS memo of 26 August 1940 "*the Nelson Column represents for England a symbol of British Naval might and world domination*". He went on to suggest that Nelson's Column should be removed and placed in Berlin. It would certainly have had an effect. Rather than subdue, it would have been more likely to provoke!

In the foreground of this postcard is 'the latest agent in modern naval warfare' - the submarine *No 3*, one of the five Holland submarines that formed the nucleus of Britain's fleet at the beginning of the twentieth century. The postcard shows HMS *Victory* in the background, an attempt by the postcard publisher to emphasise yet again the relationship between the old and the new power of the Navy. Lieutenant Max Horton captained this submarine pre-First World War, later being the first Commander to sink a German warship, the cruiser *Hela*, in the Baltic while Captain of *E9*. Max Horton, as Vice Admiral and Commander in Chief Western Approaches, went on to oversee the defeat of the U-Boats in the pivotal Battle of the Atlantic during the Second World War, and to appear on other postcards.

198. *Ready Aye Ready! - published by Rotary Photographic Co. Ltd, no. 7121Q*

This type of multi-view postcard, coupled with the use of photographs, proved useful to postcard publishers in their efforts to generate confidence in the Navy and its leaders. Using photographic imagery rather than artwork, Nelson, his Trafalgar Signal and HMS *Victory* are deliberately placed centrally on this postcard - a reflection of the perception of many that they enshrined the spirit and heart of England and were therefore central to any hope of victory in the expected conflict.

199. Newcastle Chronicle Photo, *Well over and never a Hitch. Tank Nelson at West Hartlepool - published by Sage, West Hartlepool, in their Photo Series*

As the First World War ground on, the need to finance the huge cost was, in part, met by the sale of War Bonds. As part of the promotional campaign, tanks and other war equipment were taken around the country. During the Second World War, Spitfires or shot-down German aircraft were displayed for similar reasons. World War I tank banks, as they were known, were a big draw. Large crowds were attracted, as here in West Hartlepool, where *Nelson*, one of the best-known tanks, was on display. This real photographic card is scarce. In the 1918 War Bond national fund-raising league of cities and towns, West Hartlepool came first, based on pounds raised per head of population (over £2 million). There are other postcards of Nelson the Tank published at the time, all keenly sought-after by collectors.

Inspiration and example are intended to influence the next generations. They are the hope for the future. The fashion, early in the twentieth century, of dressing boys in sailor outfits was testament to the national pride in the navy of the time, which was seen as the guardian of national security. Nelson was the embodiment of this, hence the HMS *Victory* cap.

Countless studio photographic postcards can be found of sailors and others wearing the HMS *Victory* cap band. Photographers obviously found them profitable. Few pictures, though, are as effective as this one, which is a hand-painted real photograph. Such cards were forerunners of the coloured postcards, which were printed using various processes, and then, later, produced using colour photography. While expressing the pride in Nelson and the naval tradition, it has a charm that spans generations.

Postcards are both a record of our heritage and a significant element of it. I hope this selection of postcard images has helped to highlight that in a small way. The variety of Nelson postcards retelling his story, and encouraging sacrifice and duty, undoubtedly influenced people and therefore impacted on history. The selection of 200 in this tribute to Nelson is only a small part of that very large record. There are still many more out there to find and enjoy. To quote from the HMS *Foudroyant* poem, passionately written by Sir Arthur Conan Doyle and reproduced on the next page *"there still does lie, deep in our hearts, a hungry love for what concerns our island story"*. Good luck with your collecting!

HMS *FOUDROYANT*

Who says the Nation's purse is lean,
Who fears for claim or bond or debt,
When all the glories that have been
Are scheduled as a cash asset?
If times are bleak and trade is slack,
If coal and cotton fail at last,
We've something left to barter yet
Our glorious past.

There's many a crypt in which lies hid
The dust of statesman or of king;
There's Shakespeare's home to raise a bid,
And Milton's house its price would bring.
What for the sword that Cromwell drew?
What for Prince Edward's coat of mail?
What for our Saxon Alfred's tomb?
They're all for sale!

And stone and marble may be sold
Which serve no present daily need;
There's Edward's Windsor, labelled old,
And Wolsey's palace, guaranteed.
St Clement Danes and fifty fanes,
The Tower and the Temple grounds;
How much for these? Just price them, please,
In British pounds.

You hucksters, have you still to learn,
The things which money will not buy?
Can you not read that, cold and stern
As we may be, there still does lie
Deep in our hearts a hungry love
For what concerns our island story?
We sell our work perchance our lives,
But not our glory.

Go barter to the knacker's yard
The steed that has outlived its time!
Send hungry to the pauper ward
The man who served you in his prime!
But when you touch the Nation's store,
Be broad your mind and tight your grip.
Take heed! And bring us back once more
Our Nelson's ship.

And if no mooring can be found
In all our harbours near or far,
Then tow the old three-decker round
To where the deep-sea soundings are;
There, with her pennon flying clear,
And with her ensign lashed peak high,
Sink her a thousand fathoms sheer.
There let her lie!

Sir Arthur Conan Doyle

Written in protest at the sale of HMS *Foudroyant* to a German ship-breaking firm in 1892

Bibliography

I have referred to many sources in an attempt to ensure accuracy. I hope I have been successful in achieving that. The following is not an exhaustive list but is, rather, a list of the most helpful.

The Nelson Dispatch - The Journal of the Nelson Society

The Nelson Companion, Colin White

The Nelson Encyclopaedia, Colin White

What's Left of Nelson, Leo Marriott

Horatio Nelson, Tom Pocock

Nelson, Carola Oman

Nelson's Purse, Martyn Downer

Horatio Nelson - A Catalogue of Picture Postcards, David Shannon

Nelson - An Illustrated History, National Maritime Museum: Roger Norriss, Brian Lavery, Stephen Deuchar

Nelson - A Personal History, Christopher Hibbert

Nelson and the Age of Fighting Sail, Oliver Warner

Nelson: The Life and Letters of a Hero, Roger Morriss

www.nelson-society.org.uk, the Nelson Society website

www.admiralnelson.org, the 1805 Club website

www.nmm.ac.uk, the National Maritime Museum website

www.hms-victory.com, the Official *HMS Victory* Website

Explore *HMS Victory* CD ROM Virtual Tour

Nelson Postcard Checklist
and Valuation Guide

Introduction

The bicentenary of the Battle of Trafalgar has already resulted in an increase in awareness of both Horatio Nelson and the general maritime heritage of this nation. The collecting of Nelson postcards is seeing changes, too. If the growth of interest in internet auction sites and attic clearance programmes has achieved one thing, it is to have stimulated and educated people to look again at those articles they previously saw as worthless. More of the 'hardly, or never, seen' postcards are now coming to light and are giving the Nelson collector a huge stimulus. The bicentenary and the resulting increased public awareness of Nelson in 2005 is likely to have further positive effects on the choice and quality of cards for sale and accelerate the already evident increase in numbers of new collectors.

Postcard collectors, like any other hunters, are always involved in a search for satisfaction. Their collections are usually focused on specific topics and areas of interest and the satisfaction comes from finding the unusual, the perfect and the elusive. For collectors interested in Horatio Nelson, the postcard offers a great deal. There is a great variety to track down, many fine pieces of artwork and design and the very rare items to whet the appetite and make the search an interesting journey. A checklist can indicate what is out there and act as a measure to judge collecting progress and success. It should provide a starting point for those who wish to have a sharper focus to their own Nelson postcard collection and, by indicating the known output of the variety of postcard publishers, it should help those who want to collect only the cards of certain individual postcard producers.

The important influences, events and personalities that were part of the life of Nelson became subjects for the postcard artists, designers and photographers and a significant part of the postcard output of the Golden Years at the beginning of the twentieth century. His life story was told and his achievements lauded by postcard publishers through their various postcard series. 1905, the centenary of Trafalgar and the death of Nelson, witnessed a boom in Nelson postcards and the publication of some excellent photographic cards. Nelson was an essential ingredient of the postcard production just prior to and during the First World War when he was often portrayed as the yardstick of bravery and excellence that all had to match.

It would be a mammoth volume that included all the postcards that had a Nelson link - towns, streets, pubs, hotels, mountains, lakes and so forth. Nelson's name can be found everywhere in the world. Nelson monuments, plaques and memorials can be found around Britain as well as elsewhere in the world and the postcards of Trafalgar Square alone would fill a book. I chose not to include such postcards unless they had additional significance, as, for example, when associated with the 1905 Nelson Centenary or because of their relative rarity.

There is, though, one extremely important artefact that directly links the present day to Nelson - his flagship at Trafalgar, HMS *Victory*. HMS *Victory* has been pictured on postcards, too, and by many postcard publishers over the years. She has featured on postcards throughout their history. From a sad, neglected, decaying and much altered hulk moored off Gosport, we can follow her salvation, rebuilding, restoration and importance to the navy through the postcards produced over the years. Postcards of HMS *Victory* also formed part of the various numbered Nelson series and illustrated the environment in which Nelson spent much of his service life and, moreover, in which he died. HMS *Victory* postcards are therefore an important constituent of the checklist.

This listing of over 800 Nelson postcards has drawn on previous listings and published information to do with Nelson postcards. It also includes a large number of my own postcards collected over about twenty years and others of which I am aware. The listing, in the case of numbered sets or series, highlights those missing postcards that are yet to be identified. There is a challenge for collectors here and in trying to attribute the considerable number of postcards listed under 'Unidentified Publisher'. Some contain clues as to their likely source but until there is firmer evidence they remain classified as publisher unknown.

Space has been provided for you to check off those postcards you have in your own collection. That is, of course, a major purpose of any checklist. The ultimate objective is to achieve a listing of all the Nelson cards ever published. Should you be willing to contribute to that, I would be delighted to have details of any cards you know of, as long as they are laid out as in this listing and include publisher (or the fact that the publisher is not known), exact title, number, format, colour and other attributes. It should then be possible to update the listing, giving due credit, and publish amendments in the future. For cards with no indication of publisher any other helpful identifying detail would be appreciated. Please contact the publisher for my contact details.

VALUES

Like any other postcard collector, I have a keen interest in the value of individual cards in my collection and have been frustrated by the lack of any definitive pricing information. I originally set out to include pricing information, then got cold feet and dropped the idea as I was aware of the difficulty and also of the debate that would probably follow. In the end I decided to try, not because I believe I have all the information or that all the information I am offering is faultless, but because someone has to begin the process so that the collecting of Nelson postcards can have a more stable structure in a world market accessible via the internet in addition to the traditional forums. Many dealers, in addition to selling through their shops and postcard fairs also sell online. From the point of view of the postcard collector, access to internet auction sites has made collecting easier, particularly for those who cannot easily reach major postcard fairs. The internet market,though, has produced examples of some startling variations in prices paid for similar cards, disproportionately high prices for some very common cards and overall has introduced a degree of uncertainty in terms of card values.

I read John Smith's thoughts on pricing in the introduction to his book *The Picture Postcards of Raphael Tuck & Sons* and I think he expressed the position very well. I, too, have done this with the intention of being helpful and would emphasise, too, that all values represent my own assessment of current market value and you are free to use or discard the information.

I have chosen to offer value bands rather than specific prices because that is a more accurate reflection of the way the market works. A card's value position within a band depends on detailed study of its condition and must also include any added value accrued by whether it has an interesting back. Condition particularly affects the pricing of cards in the cheaper bands where the collector has much more choice. There are also value variations within sets of cards produced by the same publisher, some cards appearing on the market less frequently and therefore commanding prices commensurate with their scarcity.

Subject matter is important and value reflects that. Postcards of HMS *Victory* and Nelson's Column have been published in great numbers and to justify anything above a basic valuation a postcard must stand out for some other reason - early publishing date, part of a set, interesting detail, limited edition, centenary association, higher quality or similar justification. Where cards are at the top of one value band or at the lower end of the next higher band I have given both band values separated by a diagonal line.

USING THE CHECKLIST

Postcards are listed alphabetically under publisher or source except for those that could not be attributed. Where that is the case postcards have been listed separately at the end under 'Unidentified Publisher'. The very large group of anonymously published postcards known as the Pictorial Post Card series are grouped at the beginning of the 'Unidentified Publisher' section.

The name and number of the postcard series and individual postcard numbers have been included when known, though many postcards are un-numbered. Titles are as they appear on the postcards.

The overwhelming majority of postcards produced throughout the last century were standard size - 140mm x 90mm or thereabout - whereas those of today tend to be larger size. These 'modern' cards are identified as such after their individual titles. Where a card or a series is oddly sized then this is noted.

Explanatory notes to help in identifying some individual cards have been included after their titles.

To indicate format and appearance, which may help with identifying individual post-cards, I have indicated whether the postcard is printed in landscape (L) or portrait (P) format and whether or not the postcard is coloured* (C), black and white (B), or sepia (S) in appearance.

* I have listed as 'coloured' any card with the addition of even one colour - for instance, a coloured frame around a black and white picture.

<table>
<thead>
<tr>
<th colspan="9" align="center">KEY</th>
</tr>
<tr>
<th colspan="4" align="center">Publisher details</th>
<th colspan="5" align="center">Postcard Details - Legend</th>
</tr>
<tr>
<th>Item No.</th>
<th colspan="2">Postcard Caption</th>
<th>Card No.</th>
<th>Landscape Portrait</th>
<th>Colour Black & White Sepia</th>
<th colspan="3">Value
1 Upto £2.50
2 £2.60 - £5.50
3 £5.60 - £12.50
4 £12.60 - £25.50
5 £25.60 plus</th>
</tr>
</thead>
<tbody>
<tr><td colspan="9">ANJO, JOSE. Antigua</td></tr>
<tr><td>1</td><td colspan="2">The Ruins of the House where Lord Nelson was Married, March 11th, 1787, Nevis</td><td>143</td><td>L</td><td>B</td><td colspan="3">3/4</td></tr>
<tr><td>2</td><td colspan="2">Nevis, WI, St John's Church, 'Figtree' where the register of marriage of Lord Nelson is kept</td><td>152</td><td>L</td><td>B</td><td colspan="3">3/4</td></tr>
<tr><td>3</td><td colspan="2">The original marriage certificate of Lord Nelson</td><td>163</td><td>L</td><td>S</td><td colspan="3">4/5</td></tr>
<tr><td colspan="9">ART AND HUMOUR PUBLISHING Co. Ltd.</td></tr>
<tr><td>1</td><td colspan="2">You're Doing The Same As Nelson Did (Sailor Prints Series)</td><td>161</td><td>P</td><td>C</td><td colspan="3">2</td></tr>
<tr><td colspan="9">BAMFORTH, J & Co</td></tr>
<tr><td>1</td><td colspan="2">Rule Britannia (1)</td><td>4775/1</td><td>P</td><td>C</td><td colspan="3">1</td></tr>
<tr><td colspan="9">BARRELL, WH</td></tr>
<tr><td>1</td><td colspan="2">HMS Victory, Anniversary of Trafalgar</td><td></td><td>L</td><td>C</td><td colspan="3">1/2</td></tr>
<tr><td colspan="9">BARTON, HARVEY & Son Ltd</td></tr>
<tr><td>1</td><td>Nelson's cot on board Victory</td><td>Modern</td><td>E60</td><td>P</td><td>C</td><td colspan="3">1</td></tr>
<tr><td>2</td><td>Captain Hardy's day cabin HMS Victory</td><td>Modern</td><td>E6R</td><td>P</td><td>C</td><td colspan="3">1</td></tr>
<tr><td>3</td><td colspan="2">Lord Nelson's bed, Castle Hotel Llandovery</td><td>1JB</td><td>P</td><td>C</td><td colspan="3">1/2</td></tr>
<tr><td>4</td><td colspan="2">HMS Victory. The Quarterdeck where Nelson fell</td><td>V1</td><td>L</td><td>C</td><td colspan="3">1</td></tr>
<tr><td>5</td><td colspan="2">HMS Victory Viewed from the Starboard Quarter</td><td>V3</td><td>L</td><td>C</td><td colspan="3">1</td></tr>
<tr><td>6</td><td colspan="2">HMS Victory. The Gingerbreads</td><td>V9</td><td>P</td><td>C</td><td colspan="3">1</td></tr>
<tr><td>7</td><td colspan="2">HMS Victory, Portsmouth Harbour. (Moonlit view by Ewart Baker)</td><td></td><td>P</td><td>C</td><td colspan="3">1</td></tr>
<tr><td colspan="9">B & B SERIES</td></tr>
<tr><td>1</td><td colspan="2">HMS Victory, Nelson's room at the George Hotel. The Victory's Cockpit</td><td></td><td>L</td><td>C</td><td colspan="3">1/2</td></tr>
<tr><td colspan="9">BEAGLES, J & Co. Ltd</td></tr>
<tr><td>1</td><td colspan="2">Lord Nelson</td><td>606B</td><td>P</td><td>B</td><td colspan="3">3</td></tr>
<tr><td>2</td><td colspan="2">Lord Nelson at prayer in his cabin on the eve of the Battle of Trafalgar</td><td>606C</td><td>P</td><td>B</td><td colspan="3">3</td></tr>
<tr><td>3</td><td colspan="2">The Victory breaking the line at the Battle of Trafalgar</td><td>606D</td><td>L</td><td>B</td><td colspan="3">1/2</td></tr>
<tr><td>4</td><td colspan="2">Battle of Trafalgar (battle plan)</td><td>606H</td><td>L</td><td>B</td><td colspan="3">3/4</td></tr>
<tr><td>5</td><td colspan="2">Battle of Trafalgar - portraits of Nelson, Collingwood, Hardy</td><td>606J</td><td>P</td><td>B</td><td colspan="3">4</td></tr>
<tr><td>6</td><td colspan="2">Souvenir of Trafalgar Day, October 21st</td><td>606K</td><td>P</td><td>B</td><td colspan="3">4</td></tr>
<tr><td colspan="9">BELL'S PHOTO Co. Ltd - J Walker & Co.</td></tr>
<tr><td>1</td><td colspan="2">HMS Victory</td><td>2090</td><td>L</td><td>C</td><td colspan="3">1</td></tr>
<tr><td colspan="9">BENNEY & SONS Ltd</td></tr>
<tr><td>1</td><td colspan="2">HMS Victory</td><td>9409</td><td>L</td><td>B</td><td colspan="3">1</td></tr>
<tr><td colspan="9">BIRN BROTHERS - Trafalgar Series 296</td></tr>
<tr><td>1</td><td colspan="2">'Twas in Trafalgar's bay ...</td><td></td><td>L</td><td>C</td><td colspan="3">2/3</td></tr>
<tr><td>2</td><td colspan="2">Along the line our signal ran ...</td><td></td><td>P</td><td>C</td><td colspan="3">2/3</td></tr>
<tr><td>3</td><td colspan="2">He cried as 'midst the fire he ran ...</td><td></td><td>L</td><td>C</td><td colspan="3">2/3</td></tr>
<tr><td>4</td><td colspan="2">At last the fatal wound ...</td><td></td><td>P</td><td>C</td><td colspan="3">2/3</td></tr>
<tr><td>5</td><td colspan="2">O'er Nelson's tomb ...</td><td></td><td>L</td><td>C</td><td colspan="3">2/3</td></tr>
<tr><td>6</td><td colspan="2">But those bright laurel leaves ...</td><td></td><td>P</td><td>C</td><td colspan="3">2/3</td></tr>
<tr><td colspan="9">BLACK, A & C - Life of Nelson, Series 1 (based on the Life of Nelson by Robert Southey)</td></tr>
<tr><td>1</td><td colspan="2">Lieutenant Nelson boarding a prize in a gale</td><td></td><td>P</td><td>C</td><td colspan="3">3</td></tr>
<tr><td>2</td><td colspan="2">Nelson loses an eye at Calvi</td><td></td><td>P</td><td>C</td><td colspan="3">3</td></tr>
<tr><td>3</td><td colspan="2">Captain Nelson in the 'Agamemnon' engaging the 'Ca Ira'</td><td></td><td>P</td><td>C</td><td colspan="3">3</td></tr>
<tr><td>4</td><td colspan="2">Nelson boarding the 'San Josef' at the battle off Cape St Vincent</td><td></td><td>P</td><td>C</td><td colspan="3">3</td></tr>
<tr><td>5</td><td colspan="2">Nelson putting the glass to his blind eye</td><td></td><td>P</td><td>C</td><td colspan="3">3</td></tr>
<tr><td>6</td><td colspan="2">Nelson at Trafalgar</td><td></td><td>P</td><td>C</td><td colspan="3">3</td></tr>
<tr><td colspan="9">BLACKMORE, JB</td></tr>
<tr><td>1</td><td colspan="2">The Last of Nelson's House, Merton</td><td></td><td>L</td><td>C</td><td colspan="3">3</td></tr>
</tbody>
</table>

KEY						

<table>
<tr><th colspan="4">Publisher details</th><th colspan="3">Postcard Details - Legend</th></tr>
<tr><th>Item No.</th><th>Postcard Caption</th><th>Card No.</th><th>Landscape Portrait</th><th>Colour Black & White Sepia</th><th colspan="2">Value
1 Upto £2.50
2 £2.60 - £5.50
3 £5.60 - £12.50
4 £12.60 - £25.50
5 £25.60 plus</th></tr>
</table>

BLUM & DEGEN Ltd

1	'Victory', Portsmouth	1382	L	B	2
2	'Victory', Portsmouth	5188	L	C	1
3	HMS Victory, Portsmouth, Flying Nelson's Signal: "England expects every man to do his duty"	10786	L	C	1

BOOTS CASH CHEMISTS Ltd

1	HMS Victory, Portsmouth	6291	P	S	1

BRITISH LIFE PUBLICATIONS

1	Nelson Collection, Monmouth. Collection of George II-George III silver presented to Lord Nelson by Friends and admirers	4052	L	B	3

BRITISH & FOREIGN SAILORS' SOCIETY

1	'Victory' in Full Sail (by G Simpson. Advertising card pub. Gale & Polden)		P	C	4

BRITISH MUSEUM

1	Last letter of Lord Nelson to Lady Hamilton 1805	25	L	B	2/3
2	Nelson's last letter	MSS3	P	B	2/3

BROWN & RAWCLIFFE Ltd

1	HMS Victory in Portsmouth Harbour		L	B	1
2	HMS Victory, Portsmouth Harbour (inset oval picturing Lord Nelson)		L	S	1
3	The 'Victory' in Portsmouth Harbour (inset oval picturing Lord Nelson)		L	C	1

BURNHAM THORPE PCC

1	Lord Nelson's Medicine Chest Modern		L	C	1

BYERS, W.E. - W.E.B. - Favourite Series

1	1805 Nelson 1905 (features HMS London)		L	C	3/4

CARWOOD PRINTING LTD

1	Nelson at Vienna 1800 by Fuger		P	C	1
2	HMS Victory off Isle of Wight 1805 by Carmichael (with Nelson's body on board) Modern		L	C	1
3	HMS Victory moored off Gosport showing The Round Tower and Sally Port in the background Modern		P	C	1

CAROUSEL INVESTACARD (Design No 8)

1	Silver Jubilee of HM Queen Elizabeth II 1977. Souvenir PC (Limited Edition)		L	C	1

CASSELL & Co Ltd (including Cassell's Art Postcards, Cassell's Saturday Journal)

1	Nelson wounded at the Battle of the Nile		P	C	2
2	Nelson at the Battle of Copenhagen		L	C	1/2
3	Nelson in his cabin on board the 'Victory'		P	C	3
4	Nelson coming on deck on the morning of Trafalgar		P	C	3
5	Men of the 'Redoubtable' trying to board the 'Victory' at the Battle of Trafalgar		P	C	2
6	The death of Nelson 1805 (after Maclise)		L	C	2
7	Greenwich pensioners at the tomb of Nelson		L	C	2
8	Trafalgar Centenary		P	C	2/3
9	Nelson's first farewell (from a painting by George W Joy)		P	C	2

CENTRO DE PROPAGANDA Y FOMENTO DEL TURISMO - printed by PVK

1	Santa Cruz de Tenerife. Historical cannon 'Tigre' ...	15928	L	B	3/4

CHARPENTIER & Co

1	View of the Harbour and HMS Victory from Clarence Square, Gosport		L	B	1/2
2	HMS Victory 1920		L	C	2/3

	KEY				
	Publisher details		**Postcard Details - Legend**		
Item No.	Postcard Caption	Card No.	**L**andscape **P**ortrait	**C**olour **B**lack & White **S**epia	Value **1** Upto £2.50 **2** £2.60 - £5.50 **3** £5.60 - £12.50 **4** £12.60 - £25.50 **5** £25.60 plus

CLWYD RECORD OFFICE

1	Emma Hamilton's Cottage, Hawarden c1870		L	B	2/3

COLEBY-CLARKE, GMH

1	Spirit of Victory		L	C	2

COLLECTORS PUBLISHING SERIES, including 'The Mercury Series'

1	Nelson's house, Merton		L	B	2/3
2	Nelson's house, Merton (different view)		L	C	2/3
3	Nelson's Bench, Merton Church		L	B	3
4	Nelson's Bench, Merton Church		L	C	3

COLOURMASTER

1	The Admiral Sir Thomas Hardy monument near Dorchester	PT2441	L	C	1
2	HMS Victory	PT2620	P	C	1

CONSTANCE, D, including New Donald McGill Comics

1	"I just popped up, me Lord, to see if you'd give me Lady Hamilton's address"	1928	P	C	2

CORBYN, JJ

1	Lest We Forget		P	B	3/4

COWELL, WS - including Christchurch Series

1	Nelson Centenary 1905 (History of Union Flag)		P	C	3

COZENS, C

1	HMS Victory in dock		L	S	2
2	HMS Victory in Portsmouth Dockyard		L	S	2/3

CRIBB, STEPHEN

1	Navy Week Portsmouth - HMS Victory and Submarine. Victory Sailing Model ...		L	S	2
2	Navy Week Portsmouth - HMS Victory. Royal Marines of the port - 'Beating the Retreat'		P	S	2/3
3	Past and Present HMS Victory and HMS Australia (green monochrome. Singer advert card)		L	C	2
4	HMS Victory and Submarine (Past and Present) B1 alongside (photo S Cribb)		L	S	1/2
5	HMS Victory (1765) Bellerephon (1909). Two famous names at Trafalgar (1805)		L	S	2
6	Past and Present. HMS Victory, Submarine No 3 steaming out of harbour for trials		L	B	2/3

DAFNIS, GL

1	2 Pierrepont St., Bath. Admiral Lord Nelson dwelt here		P	B	3

DAVIS, AM

1	England expects that every man will do his duty		P	C	3

DAVIS, J - Victoria Series

1	Walmer Castle. Nelson's Corner	990	L	B	3

DELITTLE, FENWICK & Co - including Defco Series - also see listing under SHUREY'S PUBLICATIONS

1	HMS Victory, Portsmouth		P	C	1/2
2	HMS 'Victory'		P	C	1/2

DEXTER

1	Trafalgar Square Showing Nelson's Statue, Barbados	48760-B	L	C	2/3

<table>
<tr><th colspan="7" align="center">KEY</th></tr>
</table>

	Publisher details			Postcard Details - Legend		
Item No.	Postcard Caption		Card No.	Landscape Portrait	Colour Black & White Sepia	Value: **1** Upto £2.50 / **2** £2.60 - £5.50 / **3** £5.60 - £12.50 / **4** £12.60 - £25.50 / **5** £25.60 plus

DIXON, J ARTHUR - including LFA Nelson Series 565

Item No.	Postcard Caption		Card No.	L/P	Colour	Value
1	Lord Viscount Nelson KB			P	S	2
2	Bucklers Hard. Three of Nelson's fleet built here	Modern	7713	L	C	1
3	The 'Victory' at Portsmouth, Hampshire	Modern	PHA86348	L	C	1
4	The Mary Rose and HMS Victory	Modern	PHA25875	L	C	1

DOWNEY, W & D

Item No.	Postcard Caption	Card No.	L/P	Colour	Value
1	Others Are Ready And Willing ...		P	C	3

EAS - listed under SCHWERDFEGER, EA & Co

EAST LONDON PRINTING Co

Item No.	Postcard Caption	Card No.	L/P	Colour	Value
1	Nelson (Souvenir 1805 1905)		P	C	3

ENGLISH LIFE PUBLICATIONS

Item No.	Postcard Caption	Card No.	L/P	Colour	Value
1	Lord Nelson's chair, Nelson's Collection Monmouth		L	B	2/3
2	Personal possessions of Lord Nelson, Nelson Collection, Monmouth		L	B	2/3
3	Miniature of Lord Nelson and Lady Hamilton		L	B	2/3
4	Lord Nelson's personal clothing	4054	L	B	2/3

ETTLINGER, M & Co Ltd - including Royal Series

Item No.	Postcard Caption	Card No.	L/P	Colour	Value
1	'Fordroyant' (sic). A memory of Nelson's glorious victory wrecked at Blackpool 1897	4508	L	C	3
2	'Fordroyant' (sic). A memory of Nelson's glorious victory wrecked at Blackpool 1897	4509	L	B	3
3	'Fordroyant' (sic). A memory of Nelson's glorious victory wrecked at Blackpool 1897 (different picture but same no. as 4509 above)	4509	L	S	3

EXCELSIOR FINE ARTS Co Ltd - including EFA Nelson Series 565

Item No.	Postcard Caption	Card No.	L/P	Colour	Value
1	Nelson as Vice Admiral (from a painting by Hoppner)		P	B	2/3
2	Lord Viscount Nelson, KB (semi profile facing his right)		P	B	2/3
3	Lord Viscount Nelson, KB (profile facing his left)		P	B	2/3

EYRE & SPOTTISWOODE Ltd - including Woodbury Series

Item No.	Postcard Caption	Card No.	L/P	Colour	Value
1	HMS 'Victory', Portsmouth	383	L	S	1/2
2	Nelson's Flagship The 'Victory', In Portsmouth Harbour	2075	P	S	2
3	Nelson wounded at Calvi (from a painting by Ernest Prater)	2080	P	B	3
4	Where Nelson Was Educated: Interior of Burnham Thorpe Grammar School	2082	P	S	3
5	The Church, Burnham Thorpe, of which Nelson's father was Rector	2083	L	S	3
6	Lord Nelson (for National Portrait Gallery)	3240	P	S	2/3
7	HMS 'Victory', Trafalgar Day, Portsmouth	3778	L	C	2
8	Lady Hamilton (for National Portrait Gallery)	6227	P	S	2/3
9	Lady Hamilton (for National Portrait Gallery)	6240	P	S	2/3

FANCY FARE, SOUTHSEA

Item No.	Postcard Caption	Card No.	L/P	Colour	Value
1	Viscount Nelson	2702	P	B	2

FAVOURITE SERIES - listed under Byers, W. E.

FAULKNER, CW & Co Ltd - including Historical Series No.51a, 54a, Series 585

Item No.	Postcard Caption		Card No.	L/P	Colour	Value
1	"Thank God I Have Done My Duty" (blue-bordered Gladys Storey fund raising card issued WW1. These cards are found with Union Flag or White Ensign)			P	C	3
2	Arms of Lord Nelson			P	C	3
3	Nelson's famous signal (two variations)		1457	P	C	3
4	Horatio, Viscount Nelson - painting by Lemuel Abbott (inc. Nelson mottoes)			P	C	2
5	Horatio, Viscount Nelson - painting by Lemuel Abbott		67D	P	C	2/3
6	England expects that every man will do his duty...	Series 19A		L	C	3
7	The Flags used in Nelson's Famous Signal	Series 51a		P	C	2/3
8	Horatio Nelson. Let him wear the palm who has deserved it	Series 54a		L	C	3
9	England Expects That Every Man This Day Will Do His Duty (Horatio Nelson: dates and battles)			L	C	3

	KEY					
	Publisher details			**Postcard Details - Legend**		
Item No.	Postcard Caption	Card No.	Landscape Portrait	Colour Black & White Sepia	Value **1** Upto £2.50 **2** £2.60 - £5.50 **3** £5.60 - £12.50 **4** £12.60 - £25.50 **5** £25.60 plus	

FINE ARTS PUBLISHING Co Ltd

1	Nelson leaving Portsmouth to join HMS Victory AD1805 by AC Gow RA		P	C	3/4

FRIENDS OF ENGLISH HARBOUR, The Antigua

1	Antigua's Memento of Horatio Nelson (six views with Nelson inset)		L	S	1

FRITH, F

1	House of Lords, Royal Gallery, Death of Nelson	618	L	C	2/3

FRY, AV, & Co Ltd

1	Victory Log Book	Modern	MSS93	P	B	1

GALE & POLDEN - nb. Some cards were printed in colour, black and sepia

1	Nelson's adventure with a bear 1773		P	C	1/2
2	The wounded Spanish Commodore surrendering the 'San Nicholas' to Nelson		P	C	1/2
3	Nelson volunteering to board a prize in a violent gale 1777		P	C	1
4	Nelson's conflict with a Spanish launch July 3, 1797 (after Devas)		P	C	2
5	Death of Nelson (after Devas)* (inc. 'A' Series)	6	L	B	1
6	Nelson's conflict with a Spanish launch July 3, 1797 (after Devas)	94	L	C	2
7	Here Nelson Fell		L	C	2
8	HMS Victory. Here Nelson fell. Recent visit of HM the King		P	B	2
9	Portrait of Lord Nelson		P	C	1
10	HMS 'Victory'	E/No.1/G&P/44	L	B	1
11	HMS Victory	E/No.2/G&P/45	P	B	1
12	HMS Victory. Cockpit showing original Knee where Nelson died	E/No.4/G&P/47	P	B	1
13	Forward view showing 68 pdr. Carronade	E/No.5/G&P/48	P	B	1
14	Admiral Lord Nelson	E/No.6/G&P/49	P	C	1
15	HMS Victory, Admiral Lord Nelson	E/No.6/G&P/49	P	B	1
16	HMS Victory, Death of Admiral Lord Nelson	E/No.9/G&P/52	L	B	1
17	HMS Victory, 32 Pounder Guns, Lower Gun Deck	E.No.10/G&P/53	L	B	1
18	Admiral Lord Nelson's cot	E/No.11/G&P/54	P	B	1/2
19	HMS Victory, Bow View showing Figure Head (also found without 'HMS Victory' wording on front)	E/No.12/G&P/55	P	B	1/2
20	HMS Victory, Stern Galleries at Dusk	E/No.17/G&P/82	P	B	1/2
21	HMS Victory, Nelson's Signal at Trafalgar	E/18/G & P/83	L	C	2
22	HMS Victory flying Lord Nelson's famous signal	18/G & P/83	P	C	1
23	HMS Victory Flying Lord Nelson's Famous Signal	E/No.21/G&P/199	P	C	1
24	HMS Victory Dressed Overall	E/No.22/G&P/214	L	C	1
25	HMS Victory. Gingerbreads and Admiral's Lights	E No.24/G&P/216	P	C	1
26	HMS Victory. The Quarter Deck looking aft	E.No.31/G&P/249	L	C	1
27	Nelson's prayer	E/No32/G & P/268	P	B	1/2
28	HMS Victory, Admiral Lord Nelson (also E/No6?G & P/49)	E/No. 33/G & P/275	P	B	1
29	HMS Victory. Two of the Original Guns		L	S	1
30	Two of the Trafalgar guns in HMS Victory		L	C	1
31	HMS Victory. The way they worked the guns at Trafalgar (same picture as HMS Victory Gun's Crew)		L	C	1
32	HMS Victory Gun's Crew		L	B	1
33	In the Cockpit of HMS Victory		L	C	2
34	HMS Victory. Plaque marking spot where Admiral Lord Nelson was mortally wounded - also found without 'HMS Victory' wording on front		P	B	1
35	Battle of Trafalgar. Nelson mortally wounded on the deck of HMS Victory		L	B	2
36	HMS Victory. Lord Nelson's flagship at Trafalgar		L	C	1
37	HMS Victory. Nelson's barge		L	S	2/3
38	HMS Victory (WL Wyllie)		L	C	2/3
39	HMS Victory		L	C	1
40	HMS Victory in Portsmouth Harbour		P	C	1
41	HMS Victory, after WL Wyllie		L	C	1/2
42	HMS Victory Gingerbreads and Admiral's Lights		P	B	1
43	HMS Victory. Nelson's barge	V10	L	S	1/2
44	HMS Victory from Gosport	V12	L	B	1
45	Battle of Trafalgar showing the 'Redoubtable' from which Nelson was shot		L	S	2
46	Admiral Lord Nelson by Lemuel Abbott		P	C	1/2
47	England expects that every man will do his duty (flag guide)		L	C	1/2
48	The 'Victory' sailing into action at Trafalgar (after Simpson)		P	C	1/2
49	Lord Nelson's day Cabin		L	C	1/2
50	Nelson's Famous Signal. The famous signal as hoisted on HMS 'Victory'.	1278	L	C	2/3

	KEY				
	Publisher details			**Postcard Details - Legend**	

Item No.	Postcard Caption	Card No.	Landscape Portrait	Colour Black & White Sepia	Value **1** Upto £2.50 **2** £2.60 - £5.50 **3** £5.60 - £12.50 **4** £12.60 - £25.50 **5** £25.60 plus
51	Battle of Trafalgar 1805. Nelson going into action (after E. lbbetson)	1284			2/3
52	HMS Victory. View of ship when lying in Portsmouth Harbour	2113	P	S	1
53	HMS Victory	2113	P	S	1
54	HMS Victory. View of ship when lying in Portsmouth Harbour	2114	L	S	1
55	HMS Victory. Portsmouth Harbour	2115	L	S	1
56	HMS Victory. Nelson's barge	2116	L	S	1
57	The Death of Nelson -Turner	2117	L	S	1
58	HMS Victory. Here Nelson fell	2118	P	S	1
59	HMS Victory. Here Nelson died	2119	L	S	1
60	HMS Victory Lower Mess Deck	2120	L	S	1
61	HMS Victory. Two of the Original Guns	2121	L	S	1
62	HMS Victory. Nelson's cabin	2122	L	B	1
63	HMS Victory. Aft Deck, General View	2123	L	S	1
64	Battle of Trafalgar (2.15 pm)	2124	L	B	2
65	Lord Nelson	2139	P	B	1
66	Nelson's house at Merton in 1805 (from drawing)		L	B	2
67	Temeraire engaging Redoubtable ...		L	B	2
68	HMS Victory. Cockpit showing original knee where Nelson died		L	B	1/2
69	Lord Nelson in the 'Victory' at Trafalgar, 1805		L	C	1
70	HMS Victory and Portsmouth Harbour		L	C	1
71	HMS Victory from Gosport		L	B	1
72	Here Nelson Fell		L	C	2
73	HMS Victory. Plaque marking the spot where Nelson was mortally wounded		P	B	1
74	Admiral Lord Nelson Postcard of HMS Victory Series		P	B	1
75	'The Army and Navy' from engraving by SW Reynolds after JP Knight RA (picture of Nelson and Wellington)		P	S	2
76	'Victory' leaving Portsmouth, September 1805 A Series	1	P	B	2
77	'Victory' watching the French fleet off Cadiz A Series	2	L	S	2
78	Nelson wounded A Series	5	L	B	2
79	HMS Victory, Souvenir Packet of 6 (complete in packet)	-	-	-	3
80	Battle of Trafalgar. The Destruction of the French 'Achille'		L	S	2/3
81	Battle of Trafalgar. HMS Conqueror engaging the French Flagship 'Bucentaure'		L	S	2/3
82	Battle of Trafalgar. HMS Neptune engaging the Spanish Flagship 'Santissima Trinidada'		L	S	2/3

GEISER, J   Algeria

1	Duguay-Trouin - Campagne 1905-1906 (inc. Calton Hill Monument, Edinburgh)		L	B	2

GIBSON, SM

1	England expects... (Bas-Relief of Death of Nelson at the base of Nelson's Column)		P	B	2/3

GIESEN BROTHERS & Co listed under Keliher JJ

GIEVES Ltd

1	HMS 'Victory'		P	S	1

GOOD, Henry & Son

1	"Thank God I Have Done My Duty" (red-bordered Gladys Storey fund raising card - probably a later issue than the blue-bordered version published by Faulkner)		P	C	4

GOTTSCHALK, DREYFUS & DAVIS - including GD & D 'Star' Series

1	Portrait of Nelson, From Painting in National Portrait Gallery by Henry Edridge		P	C	1
2	The Death of Nelson, by B West		L	C	1/2
3	The Death of Nelson, by Turner		L	C	1
4	Nelson volunteering to board from painting in Greenwich hospital		P	C	1
5	Portrait of Nelson, From Painting in National Portrait Gallery by SF Abbott		P	C	1
6	The Nelson monument in St Paul's Cathedral		P	C	1
7	HMS Victory (inset of Admiral Sir Archibald Douglas)		L	B	1

GUILDHALL MUSEUM

1	Nelson relics	15	L	B	2/3

GYSKA

1	The Battle of Trafalgar 1805 by Clarkson Stanfield RA		L	B	1/2

KEY						
	Publisher details			**Postcard Details - Legend**		
Item No.	Postcard Caption		Card No.	Landscape Portrait	Colour Black & White Sepia	Value **1** Upto £2.50 **2** £2.60 - £5.50 **3** £5.60 - £12.50 **4** £12.60 - £25.50 **5** £25.60 plus

HAMILTON-FISHER

1	Middle Gun Deck and Main Capstan			L	B	1
2	The Cockpit. Here Nelson Died			L	B	1
3	The Quarter Deck, where Nelson fell			L	B	1
4	Nelson's Quarters			L	B	1
5	HMS Victory Flying Trafalgar Signal			L	B	1/2

HAMMOND'S STUDIO

1	Lord Nelson's funeral procession by water from Greenwich Hospital to White-hall. Jany 8th 1806	Modern		L	B	1

HARTMANN, FREDERICK

1	HMS Victory on Trafalgar Day		1511.6	P	C	1
2	Past and Present. HMS Victory, Submarine No 3 steaming out of harbour for trials		1323	L	S	3
3	Trafalgar Square, London (Hold to Light)	Transparency series	4	L	C	3

HAUSER-Y-MENET, Madrid

1	Flags taken from Nelson (refers to Tenerife action 1797)			P	S	2

HENOCHSBERG & ELLIS

1	The Nelson Centenary, October 21st.1805-1905. Nelson Memorial, Exchange Square			P	S	2

HILDESHEIMER, S & Co Ltd

1	HMS Victory, showing Nelson's famous signal "England Expects Every Man To Do His Duty"			L	S	1
2	Brother in Arms		614	P	C	3

HINE BROS

1	The Nelson Centenary. Hardy's Monument (Portesham, Dorset)			P	S	3

HOLLOWAY WHJ

1	National War Bond Tank (Trafalgar Square 1917) nb No. 130 'Nelson'		1	L	S	4

HOLMES, OSWALD

1	Nelson Memorial, Town Hall, Pontefract			L	S	2

HOOD & Co (SanBride trademark)

1	Horatio Nelson, Viscount and Admiral AD 1758-1805			P	C	2
2	Clarence Square and Victory, Gosport			L	B	2

HOUGH, Douglas I.O.M. (San Bride trademark, so probably printed by Hood & Co.)

1	England Expects That Every Man Will Do His Duty (HMS Victory & three insets including Capt Quilliam and Kirk Arbory)			P	C	2/3

H.S., Margate

1	H.M.S. Victory in Portsmouth Harbour	Carbon Gloss Series		P	S	1

ILLUSTRATED DAILY POSTCARD, The, London E.C.

1	No. 1 Oct 21 1905 Centenary celebration. Keep Ever Green the Memory ...			P	B	5
2	No. 2 Oct 23 1905 Snap-Shots on Trafalgar Day			P	B	5

IMPERIAL FINE ART CORP.

1	Nelson at the Battle of Trafalgar by John Schonberg			L	B	2

INTER-ART Co. - including Comrade II Series

1	'Twas in Trafalgar Bay... A Glorious Record and we can play it over again		970	P	C	1/2

KEY					
Publisher details			**Postcard Details - Legend**		
Item No.	Postcard Caption	Card No.	Landscape Portrait	Colour Black & White Sepia	Value **1** Upto £2.50 **2** £2.60 - £5.50 **3** £5.60 - £12.50 **4** £12.60 - £25.50 **5** £25.60 plus
2	It's All Right My Boy, All Heroes Have Loved (features Nelson, French sub-title) Valiant Series	1119	P	C	2

ISLE OF WIGHT, UK, POSTCARD CLUB

| 1 | To commemorate the bi-centenary of the Battle of Trafalgar - 21st October 1805 (Limited Edition of 2000)   Modern | 557/2000 | L | C | 2/3 |

IVEAGH BEQUEST

| 1 | Lady Hamilton at Prayer (after Romney)   Modern | | P | S | 1 |

JARROLD & SONS Ltd

1	Lord Nelson	1991	P	C	2
2	The old rectory in which Lord Nelson was born, now demolished	2174	L	C	2
3	Lectern, made of wood from the old 'Victory' given by the Lords of the Admiralty	2175	L	C	2
4	Burnham Thorpe Church	2178	L	C	2
5	Anchor of the 'Victory', Nelson's flagship ...	2181	L	C	1
6	Viscount Horatio Nelson 1758-1805 (Famous Norwich Citizens Series)		L	S	1/2
7	Viscount Horatio Nelson 1758-1805 (Famous Norwich Citizens Series) Modern		L	S	1/2
8	Horatio, Viscount Nelson 1758-1805 by JF Rigaud (1742-1810)	100	P	B	2
9	The grave of Admiral Lord Nelson in the Crypt St Paul's	CKSTP1	P	C	2
10	Wax effigy. Admiral Nelson		P	B	2/3
11	Nelson's Prayer on the eve of Trafalgar		P	C	2/3

JONES, AVN & Co

| 1 | England expects that every man will do his duty | | L | C | 2/3 |

JONES, HH

| 1 | West-Park, Wolverhampton (floral display.. 'England expects ...') | | L | S | 5 |

JONES, P

| 1 | Souvenir of Nelson Centenary (with additional verse to the *Death of Nelson*) | | L | C | 3/4 |

JONES, SE

| 1 | Nelson Centenary 1805-1905. Birthplace of England's great naval hero Horatio Viscount Nelson, Parsonage home ... | | L | B | 4 |

KELIHER, JJ Co Ltd - including Giesen Brothers, some Woolstone Brothers inc. Milton 'Life of Nelson' Series 560

1	Vice-Admiral Lord Collingwood 1750-1810 Admirals All Series	8	P	C	2/3
2	Horatio, Viscount Nelson 1758-1805 Admirals All Series	10	P	C	2
3	Sir Thomas Hardy (Nelson's Hardy) Admirals All Series	11	P	C	2/3
4	Battle of Trafalgar, HMS 'Victory' Oct 21st 1805		P	C	1
5	"England expects every man this day will do his duty" Topical Series	10	L	C	2/3
6	Lord Nelson wounded at the Nile Aug lst 1798		P	C	2
7	Commodore Nelson boarding the San Nicolas February 14th 1797		P	C	1/2
8	Commodore Nelson boarding the 'San Josef' February 14th 1797		P	C	1
9	Horatio Nelson, Midshipman 1773. Adventure with a bear		L	C	2
10	Rear Admiral Nelson's conflict with a Spanish launch July 3rd 1797		P	C	2
11	Lieut. Nelson volunteering to board a prize in a violent gale Nov 20 1777	2065	P	C	1
12	Sir Horatio Nelson wounded at Tenerife July 24th 1797	2066	P	C	2
13	Lord Nelson mortally wounded, Oct 21st 1805	2067	P	C	2
14	Rear Admiral Lord Nelson KB, 1798	2072	P	C	1
15	Flags used by Lieut Pasco HMS 'Victory' for Lord Nelson's signal at Trafalgar		P	C	3
16	Vice Admiral Viscount Nelson KB		P	C	1
17	Battle of the Nile, August 1st, 1798		L	C	2
18	HMS Victory, Portsmouth Arlette Series	108	P	C	1
19	HMS Victory Glazette Series	1080	P	C	1
	* Some of these cards, including nos. 4, 6, 11, 12, 13, 16 and 17 can also be found published by Giesen Bros and Woolstone Bros, the latter in 'Milton' series 560 'Life of Nelson'.				

KILTO, FRED

| 1 | Nelson's prayer | | P | S | 2/3 |

	Publisher details				Postcard Details - Legend			
Item No.	Postcard Caption		Card No.	Landscape Portrait	Colour Black & White Sepia	Value		
						1 Upto £2.50 **2** £2.60 - £5.50 **3** £5.60 - £12.50 **4** £12.60 - £25.50 **5** £25.60 plus		

KINGSWAY - see Smith, WH

KNIGHT BROS - including Kelkel Series (also see ROYAL UNITED SERVICE MUSEUM)

		Card No.	L/P	Col	Value
1	Horatio Viscount Nelson 1758-1805	1275	P	C	1
2	HMS 'Victory', Trafalgar Day	1447	L	B	1/2
3	Nelson in his cabin	1448	P	B	3
4	HMS Victory The Upper Deck	1449	L	B	2
5	HMS Victory Portsmouth. Facsimile of tablet let into wall of George Hotel	1450	P	B	3
6	HMS Victory The Ward Room	1451	L	B	1
7	HMS 'Victory's Anchor (also with Christmas & New Year message on reverse)	1452	L	B	1
8	The Nelson Centenary 1905	1465	P	C	2/3
9	The Nelson Centenary, The Nelson Celebrations in Trafalgar Square, London, October 21st, 1905 (also a 2nd edition)	1724	P	B	3/4
10	Naval Scotch Pipers of HMS Victory Dainty Novels Series		P	S	1/2
11	Barbados. The Nelson Monument (Series of 24)	10	L	B	4

LANSDOWNE PUBLISHING Co Ltd

		Card No.	L/P	Col	Value
1	Training Ship Foudroyant & Harbour Entrance, Gosport (formerly Trincomalee)	LP 72	L	B	1

LEDER, OTTO, Barbados

		Card No.	L/P	Col	Value
1	Trafalgar Day, Barbados 1905, Nelson's statue	178:07	L	B	4

LEON & LEVY (LL)

		Card No.	L/P	Col	Value
1	Portsmouth. - The Victory	7	L	C	1
2	Portsmouth. The George Hotel in which Nelson spent his last hours in England	11	L	B	3
3	London, St Paul's Cathedral - The Monument of Lord Nelson	161	P	B	1

LILYWHITE Ltd

			L/P	Col	Value
1	The Viscountess Nelson Tomb, Littleham		L	S	3

LONDON TOURIST BORED (sic) - Comic card

			L/P	Col	Value
1	Nelson takes a fall		L	C	3

LOOSEMORE

			L/P	Col	Value
1	In memory of England's Hero		P	C	2/3

LOSADA, A MOURE, Basseterre, St. Kitts

		Card No.	L/P	Col	Value
1	St John's Church, Figtree, Nevis (Where Lord Nelson's Marriage Certificate is kept)	60A	L	S	4/5
2	Original marriage certificate of Lord Nelson	61a	L	B	4/5
3	Original marriage certificate of Lord Nelson (reprint)	1058	L	B	4/5
4	Interior of 'Figtree' Church, Nevis, where Lord Nelson's marriage certificate is kept	88a	L	B	4
5	Ruins of marriage place of Lord Nelson, Nevis, WI	104A	P	B	4

LOVERING & Co

			L/P	Col	Value
1	Effigy of Lord Nelson 1805, Westminster Abbey		P	C	2

MACK, E

		Card No.	L/P	Col	Value
1	Past and present (Nelson and WWI Dreadnought)	598	P	C	2
2	England expects that every man will do his duty 1915	654	L	C	2

MAHOMET, AJ

			L/P	Col	Value
1	Nelson Rectory Burnham Thorpe		L	B	4

MARINE-GALERIE

		Card No.	L/P	Col	Value
1	Engl. Dreidecker 'Victory'	42	P	C	3

McLINTOCH

			L/P	Col	Value
1	Lady Hamilton (Plant Ash Soap 4 - Series 1)		P	C	4

	Publisher details		Postcard Details - Legend		
Item No.	Postcard Caption	Card No.	Landscape Portrait	Colour Black & White Sepia	Value **1** Upto £2.50 **2** £2.60 - £5.50 **3** £5.60 - £12.50 **4** £12.60 - £25.50 **5** £25.60 plus

MEDICI SOCIETY

1	Viscount Nelson, Viscounte Nelson (after Abbott)	31	P	C	2
2	Lady Hamilton Romney	196	P	C	2
3	Lady Hamilton with a goat (after Romney)	48	P	C	1/2
4	Lady Hamilton (after Romney. Tennant Collection)	66	P	C	1/2

MERCURY SERIES listed under Collectors Publishing Co

MERTON LIBRARY SERVICE

1	Merton Abbey		L	B	3
2	St Mary's Church, Merton		L	B	3

MIDDLEBROOK

1	Silver Dishes and Gold Knee Buckles		L	B	3/4

MILLAR & LANG Ltd - including National Series

1	HMS Victory in Portsmouth Dockyard		L	B	1
2	HMS Victory in Portsmouth Dockyard		L	C	1
3	HMS Victory Flying Nelson's Signal		P	C	1

MILLS & Co

1	HMS Victory. Model Boat, Exact Copy Built In Portsmouth Dockyard	308	L	S	1
2	HMS Victory. Portsmouth Dockyard	625	P	S	1
3	HMS Victory. Portsmouth Dockyard, Lord Nelson's famous flagship. A view showing ...	625	P	S	1/2
4	HMS Victory and Modern Submarines, Portsmouth Dockyard	626	P	S	1/2

MILLS, John W - including some Woolstone's 'Milton'-trademarked cards

1	HMS Victory showing Nelson's famous signal "England Expects ..."	51435	L	C	1/2
2	HMS 'Victory', Portsmouth Harbour		L	C	1
3	HMS Victory Flying Nelson's Signal		L	C	1
4	HMS Victory Portsmouth		P	C	1
5	HMS Victory. Ships, Portsmouth		L	B	2

MISCH & Co. - inc. Misch & Stock Cards 1-15 'Nelson Centenary Series' 2 sets inc. re-issues?

1	Lord Nelson	316/1	P	C	1
2	HMS Victory, The Anchor on Southsea Esplanade	316/2	L	C	1
3	HMS Victory. The Quarter Deck	316/3	L	C	1
4	HMS Victory flying Nelson's famous signal	316/4	L	C	1
5	HMS Victory. The Upper Deck	316/5, 67615	L	C	2
6	HMS Victory. The Main Deck	316/6	L	C	1
7	Nelson's Flagship Foudroyant wrecked at Blackpool 1897 (different picture to 13 below)	316/6, 54253	L	C	3/4
8	HMS Victory. The Quarter Deck	316/8, 67389	L	C	1/2
9	HMS Victory Flying Nelson's famous signal	317/7, 67393	P	C	1/2
10	HMS Victory. The Main Deck	317/8, 67618	L	C	1/2
11	HMS Victory. The Cock Pit	317/9, 54256	P	C	1/2
12	The Battle of Trafalgar from the painting by Stanfield in Royal United Service Club	31710, 67620	L	C	1/2
13	Nelson's Flagship Foudroyant wrecked at Blackpool 1897 (different picture to 7 above)	317/1, 54258	L	C	3/4
14	Nelson's Flagship Foudroyant showing damaged hull wrecked at Blackpool 1897	317/1, 67398	L	C	3/4
15	HMS Victory. The Quarter Deck	67613	L	C	1/2
16	The Cathedral of the Navy. HMS Victory, Portsmouth Dockyard	140	L	S	2
17	Walmer Castle. Nelson received Here his instructions for the Battle of Trafalgar	237	L	C	3
18	The Death of Nelson (D MacLise RA) Imperial Frescoes Series	311	L	C	1/2
19	The Death of Nelson (after Turner) Great Masters Series	442	L	C	1/2
20	HMS Victory and Modern Submarines. Portsmouth Dockyard	626	P	S	2

MITCHELL & WATKINS - including Canon Series

1	Nelson Day Trafalgar Square (1905)		L	B	4
2	Nelson Day		L	B	3

	KEY					

<table>
<tr><th colspan="3">Publisher details</th><th colspan="4">Postcard Details - Legend</th></tr>
</table>

Item No.	Postcard Caption		Card No.	Landscape Portrait	Colour Black & White Sepia	Value 1 Upto £2.50 / 2 £2.60 - £5.50 / 3 £5.60 - £12.50 / 4 £12.60 - £25.50 / 5 £25.60 plus

MODERN SERIES listed under Russell, WW & Co

MONMOUTH DISTRICT COUNCIL - including Nelson Museum Monmouth

No.	Caption		Card No.	L/P	Col	Val
1	Horatio Viscount Nelson, Duke of Bronte (aged 43) (after Hoppner)			P	C	1
2	Rear Admiral Sir Horatio Nelson KB from a print by Baxter of the portrait by Lemuel Abbott in 1797, Nelson was 39			P	C	3
3	Britannia bringing her dead hero to Britannia's shores (contemporary cartoon 1806)			L	C	1
4	Personal possessions of Lord Nelson and model of a ship of his fleet (see English Life Publications No. 2)		4056	L	B	3
5	John Bull taking a lunch from the caricature (of Nelson)	Modern		L	C	1
6	The death of Admiral Lord Nelson, etching by James Gilray	Modern		P	C	1
7	Sensibility (Lady Hamilton from an engraving 1789)	Modern		P	C	1
8	Lord Nelson's funeral procession by water	Modern		L	C	1
9	Model of Battle of Trafalgar	Modern		L	B	1
10	The Naval Temple and Round House on the Kymin, Monmouth	Modern		L	C	1
11	Model of HMS Victory as she was when Nelson knew her	Modern		P	C	1
12	Britons! Your Nelson Is Dead!...Part of a poster produced in 1806	Modern		L	B	1

MOODY, CR & Co

No.	Caption		Card No.	L/P	Col	Val
1	1805 Nelson Centenary 1905. Foes Once - Friends Now Entente Cordiale			P	C	2/3
2	Merton Abbey, Series 207			L	C	3

MORGAN, FC & Co

No.	Caption		Card No.	L/P	Col	Val
1	Nelson's Quarter Deck walk, Merton Abbey		207-4	L	C	4

M S Ltd listed under National Portrait Gallery

NATIONAL GALLERY, Millbank

No.	Caption		Card No.	L/P	Col	Val
1	Lady Hamilton. Romney		312	P	B	2/3
2	Death of Nelson (after Turner CXVI)		480	L	B	1
3	Spiritual form of Nelson (after Blake)		3006	P	B	3

NATIONAL MARITIME MUSEUM, published by HMSO - including George Pulman and Sons, Printer

No.	Caption		Card No.	L/P	Col	Val
1	Vice Admiral Sir Thomas Masterman Hardy, 1769-1839. Richard Evans, 1784-1871		11	P	S	2
2	Vice Admiral Lord Nelson 1758-1805		41	P	S	2
3	The Victory leaving Spithead, 1791 Robert Dodd 1748-1815		51	L	S	2
4	Vice Admiral Lord Nelson 1758-1805 (after Hoppner)			P	C	2
5	Admiral Lord Nelson by Lemuel Abbott			P	C	1/2
6	Rear Admiral Sir Horatio Nelson KB painted at Greenwich in 1797 after losing his right arm at Tenerife (after LF Abbott)	Modern	153	P	C	1
7	Horatio, Viscount Nelson (after LF Abbott)	Modern	153	P	C	1
8	The Victory at Trafalgar (after Turner)	Modern	156	L	C	1
9	Horatio, Viscount Nelson KB (after LF Abbott)	Modern	159	P	C	1
10	Portrait known as Lady Hamilton as Ariadne (after Romney)	Modern	160	P	C	1
11	HMS Victory at sea 1793 (after Monamy Swaine)	Modern	166	L	C	1
12	Nelson mortally wounded at Trafalgar (after D Dighton)	Modern	194	L	C	1
13	Horatio, Viscount Nelson 1758-1805 in the uniform of Post Captain 1781 (after JF Rigaud)	Modern	242	L	C	1
14	The Death of Nelson (after AW Devis)	Modern	260	L	C	1
15	Lord Nelson's signal at Trafalgar (very large format 8' x 5')	Modern	273	L	C	1
16	The destruction of the L'Orient at the Battle of the Nile (by George Arnald) 1763-1841	Modern		L	C	1
17	The Hero Of The Nile by James Gillray (1757-1815)	Modern		P	C	1
18	Nelson by Johann Heinrich Schmidt (1749-1828)	Modern		P	C	1
19	Frances, Viscountess Nelson (1761-1831) 'Nelson's wife, by an unknown artist'	Modern		P	C	1
20	Emma by Johann Heinrich Schmidt (1749-1828)	Modern		P	C	1
21	Lady Emma Hamilton by Johann Heinrich Schmidt (1749-1828)	Modern		P	C	1
22	The Battle of Trafalgar by Joseph Mallord William Turner (1775-1851)	Modern		L	C	1
23	The Battle of Trafalgar, 21 October 1805 by Joseph Mallord William Turner (1775-1851)	Modern		L	C	1
24	Horatio, Viscount Nelson, KB Vice-Admiral of the Fleet (Oil Painting by LF Abbott 1760-1803)	Modern	ENT-20	P	C	1
25	Lord Nelson's signal at Trafalgar (approx 6" x 4")	Modern	ENT-32	P	C	1
26	Face of a Hero	Modern		P	C	1
27	Lady Emma Hamilton as Ariadne, by George Romney (1734 - 1802)	Modern		P	C	1

<table>
<thead>
<tr><th colspan="3" rowspan="2"></th><th></th><th colspan="3">Postcard Details - Legend</th></tr>
<tr><th></th><th>Landscape Portrait</th><th>Colour Black & White Sepia</th><th>Value
1 Upto £2.50
2 £2.60 - £5.50
3 £5.60 - £12.50
4 £12.60 - £25.50
5 £25.60 plus</th></tr>
</thead>
</table>

KEY						

Publisher details | **Postcard Details - Legend**

Item No.	Postcard Caption		Card No.	Landscape Portrait	Colour Black & White Sepia	Value
28	The Immortality of Nelson by Sir Benjamin West (1738 -1820) 'The hero offered up to Britannia by Neptune'	Modern		P	C	1
29	Nelson's undress uniform coat, worn at the battle of Trafalgar	Modern		P	C	1
30	A colour drawing made in around 1802-3 of Nelson's daughter, Horatia...	Modern		P	C	1
31	Captain Horatio Nelson, 1758-1805 by John Francis Rigaud	Modern		P	C	1
32	Rear Admiral Sir Horatio Nelson (1758 -1805) by Lemuel Francis Abbott (1760-1803)	Modern		P	C	1
33	Burnham Thorpe. Nelson's birthplace by Francis Pocock	Modern		L	C	1
34	The British Fleet under Rear Admiral Nelson at anchor in the Bay of Naples, 17th June 1798	Modern		L	C	1
35	Extirpation of the Plagues of Egypt - Destruction of Revolutionary Crocodiles	Modern		L	C	1
36	Admiral Lord Nelson, by Ralph Stedman	Modern		P	C	1
37	Nelson mortally wounded at Trafalgar	Modern	ENT 30	L	C	1

NATIONAL PORTRAIT GALLERY - including cards printed by various firms

1	Horatio Nelson (after Abbott)	10.16 MS No. 31		P	C	2
2	Horatio Nelson, Viscount Nelson 1758-1805 (after Abbott)	Modern	139	P	B	2
3	Horatio Nelson, Viscount Nelson 1758-1805 (after Abbott)	Modern	394	P	C	2
4	Sir William Hamilton 1730-1803 (after Reynolds)	Modern	680	P	C	2
5	Emma, Lady Hamilton 1761?-1815 (after Romney)	Modern	4448	P	C	2
6	Horatio Nelson, Viscount Nelson 1758-1805 (after G Head)	Modern	5101	P	C	2
7	Horatio Nelson, Viscount Nelson 1758-1805 (after W Beechey)	Modern	L129	P	C	2
8	HMS Victory			P	B	2

NAVY LEAGUE - including cards printed by R Tuck and Andrews & Co

1	Thank God I have done my duty			P	S	3
2	The Nelson Column, Trafalgar Square decorated by the Navy League on Trafalgar Day (Oct 21st)			P	B	4
3	Nelson Column decorated on 21st October, by the Navy League			P	B	4
4	Horatio, Viscount Nelson 1758-1805			P	C	1/2

NELSON MUSEUM MONMOUTH listed under Monmouth District Council

NELSON SOCIETY, The

1	"Nelson's reception by Sir John Jervis after the Battle of St Vincent 14th February 1797" (after AD M'Cormick)	Modern	1	L	C	1/2
2	"The Battle of Trafalgar: Nelson receives his death wound on board the Victory" (after Paul-Leon Jazet)		2	L	C	1/2

NEVIS PHILATELIC BUREAU - stamp reproductions on postcards

1	HMS Boreas off Nevis	Modern	NPH028	L	C	2
2	Lord Nelson and HMS Boreas at anchor off Nevis	Modern	NPH029	L	C	2
3	Nesbit Plantation (Fanny Nesbit's family estate)	Modern	NPHQ6	L	C	2

NORFOLK NELSON MUSEUM

1	Portrait of Horatio, Viscount Nelson 1801 (by Sir William Beechey)	Modern		P	C	1
2	The Hero of the Nile, 1798 (after James Gillray)	Modern	6	P	C	1
3	Funeral procession outside St Paul's	Modern	7	L	C	1
4	The Grand Funeral Procession	Modern	8	L	C	1
5	Lord Nelson - Oil on Canvas (after Sir M Keymer)	Modern		P	C	1

NORTH CREAKE PHOTO LIMITED

1	All Saints Parish Church with the *Lord Nelson* Inn sign, Burnham Thorpe, Norfolk	Modern		P	C	1

NORTH WALES ADVT CO, RHYL

1	Nelson's Old Flagship 'Foudroyant' wrecked at Blackpool, June 16th 1897			L	C	3/4

OPIE Ltd, Redruth

1	Implacable (formerly Duguay Trouin, a Trafalgar ship. RP)		534	L	S	3/4

<table>
<tr><td colspan="7" align="center">**KEY**</td></tr>
<tr><td colspan="4" align="center">**Publisher details**</td><td colspan="3" align="center">**Postcard Details - Legend**</td></tr>
</table>

Item No.	Postcard Caption		Card No.	Landscape Portrait	Colour Black & White Sepia	Value **1** Upto £2.50 **2** £2.60 - £5.50 **3** £5.60 - £12.50 **4** £12.60 - £25.50 **5** £25.60 plus
PAGEANTRY POSTCARDS						
1	Trafalgar 1805 - 2005		JEF 025	L	C	1
PAMLIN PRINTS						
1	Lord Nelson		C9604	P	B	1
PEARKS TEA						
1	Battle of Trafalgar			L	C	3
PHILLIPS, Godfrey Ltd						
1	Lady Hamilton With Goat (after Romney. Series of 26 given away with deliveries) 89mm x 127mm		21	P	C	2
PHOTOCROM Ltd - including Celesque Series						
1	HMS Victory. Here Nelson fell		65142	L	B	2
2	St Paul's Cathedral. Nelson's Tomb		78739	L	S	1
3	HMS Victory, The Ship's Figurehead		G5139	P	B	1
4	HMS Victory. The Stern		G5143	P	B	1
5	HMS Victory, The Foremast		V11	P	S	1
6	HMS Victory, The Masts, rigging and quarter davits		V13	P	S	1
7	HMS Victory, The Deck, Showing the Boats and Belfry		V678	P	S	1
8	HMS Victory, The Ship's Pumps		V682	L	S	1
9	Portsmouth: HMS Victory		G34301	P	C	2
10	HMS Thunderer (comic card, sailor playing and singing to *The Death of Nelson*)		582	P	C	1
PHOTO PRECISION Ltd						
1	HMS Victory	Modern	PT2617	L	C	1
2	HMS Victory	Modern	PT2621	L	C	1
3	HMS Victory	Modern	PT2623	P	C	1
4	HMS Victory Flying Lord Nelson's Famous Signal	Modern	PT2646	P	C	1
5	HMS Victory	Modern	PT3089	P	C	1
6	HMS Victory, Portsmouth	Modern	1590	L	S	1
PICTORIAL STATIONERY Co Ltd						
1	Portsmouth. 'The Victory'			L	C	1
PITKIN PICTORIALS Ltd - including Topical Press						
1	HMS Victory The Lower Gun Deck	Modern	VIC 2	L	C	1
2	Horatio, 1st Viscount Nelson (after Hoppner)	Modern	VIC 3	P	C	1
3	Nelson's Trafalgar Uniform	Modern	VIC6/80/5	P	C	1
4	HMS Victory, Nelson's cot	Modern	VIC 12	L	C	1
5	HMS Victory. ''Splice the mainbrace' was an order...	Modern	VIC 16	L	C	1
6	HMS Victory, Portsmouth Dockyard: Nelson's flagship at the Battle of Trafalgar (1805)...	Modern	NAT5/79/5	P	C	1
7	The Apotheosis of Nelson by Benjamin West	Modern	NAT6/79/5	P	C	1
8	Nelson wounded after leading attack on mole at Teneriffe on 24th July 1797 (after Westall)	Modern	NAT10/79/5	P	C	1
9	Maritime Museum, Buckler's Hard, Hampshire Detailed Model of Buckler's Hard Village in 1803	Modern	BUC14	L	C	1
PLIMMER, G.A.						
1	Nelson Monument, Barbados		8	L	C	3
POST OFFICE, British Post Office - printed by Questa						
1	Lord Nelson/HMS Victory (picture of 24p stamp issued as part of the Maritime Heritage set (16 June 1982)		PHQ60(C) 6/82	L	C	2
POST-CARD SALUTE Co.						
1	HMS Victory			L	B	1

KEY						
Publisher details				**Postcard Details - Legend**		
Item No.	Postcard Caption		Card No.	Landscape Portrait	Colour Black & White Sepia	Value **1** Upto £2.50 **2** £2.60 - £5.50 **3** £5.60 - £12.50 **4** £12.60 - £25.50 **5** £25.60 plus
POUTEAU, E.						
1	Mecklenburg Sq Gardens (floral display .... 'Nelson 1805')			L	S	5
POWELL'S, Swanage						
1	52 ft HMS Victory in Swanage Bay Sept. 1932			L	S	3
PREMIER PENNY POSTCARDS						
1	HMS Victory, Portsmouth			L	C	2
PRICES CANDLES - nb Trade Cards						
1	Battle of the Nile, August 1st 1798			L	C	3
2	Trafalgar, Oct. 21st, 1805			L	C	3
PRIVETT, Southsea						
1	Submarine and Victory			L	C	1/2
PUBLIC RECORD OFFICE						
1	Signature of Nelson			L	B	3
2	Log of the Victory (21st October 1805)		6	L	B	3/4
QUESTA - see Post Office						
RAITHBY, LAWRENCE & Co listed under National Portrait Gallery						
RAPID PHOTO PRINTING Co Ltd						
1	Portsmouth. The Victory		V255-3	L	B	1
RECKITT & SONS - *nb. Reward Card*						
1	Horatio Nelson			L	C	2
REID BROS						
1	The Death of Nelson (lines of music)			L	C	2
2	Heart of Oak (including picture of HMS Victory)			L	C	2
RICHARDSON, HENRY						
1	Lord Nelson's funeral car in Painted Hall, Greenwich			L	B	3
RICHARDSON & Co including Titchfield Series						
1	England Expects every Man To Do His Duty…And We'll All Do It		547	P	C	2
RICHTER, C. London						
1	London. Bombers Over Trafalgar Square		84233	P	C	1
RIDLEY, MJ						
1	The Victory, Portsmouth		4403	L	C	1
ROBBE, GEORGE						
1	Admiral Lord De Saumarez 1757-1837 Battle of St. Vincent 14/2/1797	Modern		L	C	2
2	Admiral Lord De Saumarez 1757-1837 Battle of the Nile 1/8/1798	Modern		L	C	2
ROBERTS & Co, Barbados						
1	Statue of Lord Nelson, Barbados			P	B	2/3
ROBERTS & WRATE Ltd - including Mason's Alpha Series						
1	Portsmouth, HMS Victory, Portsmouth dockyard		SPS13	L	B	2

Item No.	Postcard Caption	Card No.	Landscape Portrait	Colour Black & White Sepia	Value 1 Upto £2.50 2 £2.60 - £5.50 3 £5.60 - £12.50 4 £12.60 - £25.50 5 £25.60 plus
Publisher details			**Postcard Details - Legend**		

ROTARY PHOTOGRAPHIC Co Ltd

Item No.	Postcard Caption	Card No.	L/P	Colour	Value
1	Lord Nelson	N1	P	B	1
2	Conflict with a Spanish Launch, Nelson	N2	L	B	3
3	Battle of the Nile, Nelson	N3	L	B	2
4	Battle of Trafalgar, Nelson	N4	L	B	2
5	Death of Nelson	N5	L	B	2
6	The Cockpit of 'Victory', Nelson	N6	L	B	2
7	Lord Nelson	69A	P	B	3
8	1805 Souvenir 1905 Nelson	5157A	L	B	3/4
9	Ready, Aye, Ready "England Expects That Every Man Will Do His Duty"	7121Q	P	S	1/2
10	Ready, Aye, Ready	D35	P	S	1/2
11	HMS Victory	3970A	L	B	1/2
12	HMS Victory	3970B	P	B	1/2
13	Britain's "Dreadnought" of the Past ...Britain's "Dreadnought" of the To-day	GT11a	L	B	3

ROTH, T

Item No.	Postcard Caption	Card No.	L/P	Colour	Value
1	Nelson Centenary Celebrations (Liverpool)		P	S	4/5

ROSS, Berlin

Item No.	Postcard Caption	Card No.	L/P	Colour	Value
1	"Lady Hamilton" Der Grosse Millionenfilm Seeschlacht Bei Trafalgar	648/11	L	S	2/3

ROYAL NATIONAL LIFEBOAT INSTITUTION - Blackpool Branch (SanBride trademark; printed by Hood & Co.)

Item No.	Postcard Caption	Card No.	L/P	Colour	Value
1	Wreck of the Foudroyant (Froma photograph taken from the beach of the stranded ship watched by a crowd)		L	B	4
2	Wreck of the Foudroyant (Art card showing lifeboat approaching the ship. Branch details on reverse)		L	B	4

ROYAL NAVY MUSEUM TRADING COMPANY

Item No.	Postcard Caption	Card No.	L/P	Colour	Value
1	Battle of Trafalgar 2.45pm from a painting by William Bishop Modern		L	C	1

ROYAL UNITED SERVICE MUSEUM (including printing by Gale & Polden and Knight Bros)

Item No.	Postcard Caption	Card No.	L/P	Colour	Value
1	Model of HMS 'Foudroyant' (printed by Gale & Polden)		L	B	2
2	Lord Nelson's Fighting Sword ...(and four other items) (printed by Knight Bros)		P	S	4
3	Portions of the 'Victory's' Mainmast ... (and three other items) (printed by Knight Bros)		P	S	4

ROYAL SERIES listed under Ettlinger, M & Co Ltd

R.S. ART PRESS Ltd - Ruskin Studios

Item No.	Postcard Caption	Card No.	L/P	Colour	Value
1	HMS Mars at Trafalgar (painted by A Chidley)		P	C	3
2	HMS Victory (painted by A Chidley)		P	C	1/2

RUDDOCK Ltd

Item No.	Postcard Caption	Card No.	L/P	Colour	Value
1	HMS Hannibal, HMS Victory		L	C	1

RUSSELL, J & Sons

Item No.	Postcard Caption	Card No.	L/P	Colour	Value
1	Lord Nelson's Dining Cabin, HMS Victory		L	B	1/2
2	The Cockpit, HMS Victory (Here Nelson died)		L	S	1/2

RUSSELL, WW & Co

Item No.	Postcard Caption	Card No.	L/P	Colour	Value
1	England expects that every man this day will do his duty		P	C	2

RYMAN Ltd

Item No.	Postcard Caption	Card No.	L/P	Colour	Value
1	Lord Nelson's prayer before Trafalgar		P	B	2/3

SAGE

Item No.	Postcard Caption	Card No.	L/P	Colour	Value
1	'Newcastle Chronicle' Photo. Well over and never a hitch. Tank Nelson at West Hartlepool (RP. Other view also)		L	B	5
2	A Slight Leap		L	B	5
3	Standing on the Tank are...and the Mayor of Hartlepool		C	B	5
4	The Tank Nelson at West Hartlepool. Ready for record breaking		L	B	5

	Publisher details			Postcard Details - Legend		
Item No.	Postcard Caption		Card No.	Landscape Portrait	Colour Black & White Sepia	Value **1** Upto £2.50 **2** £2.60 - £5.50 **3** £5.60 - £12.50 **4** £12.60 - £25.50 **5** £25.60 plus

SALMON, J Ltd

1	Dreadnoughts New & Old		598	P	C	2/3
2	England Expects That Every Man Will Do His Duty (flag signal)		654	L	C	2/3
3	Frigate 'Foudroyant' at Portsmouth Harbour			L	B	1
4	Overy Staithe	Modern	20	L	C	2
5	The Burnhams - Nelson Country	Modern	21	L	C	1
6	Lord Nelson	Modern	507	P	C	1
7	The Victory, Portsmouth (John H Fry)		3443	P	C	3
8	The Victory, Portsmouth (John H Fry)		3444	P	C	3
9	HMS Victory flying Nelson's famous signal, as flown at the Battle of Trafalgar, 1805 (John H Fry)		3885	L	C	3
10	The Victory. Portsmouth Harbour (AR Quinton)		1102	L	C	1/2
11	England Expects That Every Man Will Do His Duty. Entrance to Portsmouth Harbour (AR Quinton)		1104	L	C	2/3
12	The Victory. Portsmouth Harbour "England Expects That Every man Will Do # His Duty" (AR Quinton)		1105	L	C	2
13	The Victory, Portsmouth Harbour (W Fred Mitchell)		1106 3132	P	C	1
14	Trafalgar Oct 21st 1805 (after John H Fry)		4300	L	C	3
15	Nelson and Trafalgar 200th Anniversary 1805 -2005	Modern		L	C	1

SCHWERDTFEGER, EA & Co - including E.A.S.

1	The death of Nelson October 21st 1805 at the Battle of Trafalgar on board the Victory (after Turner)	8204/3	L	S	2
2	HMS Victory Flying Nelson's Famous Signal	053	L	S	1/2
3	HMS Victory (Royal yacht 'Victoria and Albert' in background)	0350	L	S	2/3

SELLICK

1	Britannia Triumphant (Title of a contemporary poster regarding outcome of Trafalgar)		P	B	3

SENIOR & CO

1	Nelson's Flagship HMS Victory In Portsmouth Harbour		L	C	1

SHARPE, WN Ltd

1	Admiral Lord Nelson 1758-1805 (Classic All British Series)	226	P	C	3

SHELL nb. Trade Card

1	Horatio Nelson (1758-1805) - Great Britons Series 1972		L	C	1

SHOESMITH & ETHERIDGE Ltd

1	HMS Victory, Portsmouth Dockyard	D16860	L	B	1

SHUREYS PUBLICATIONS - including Delittle, Fenwick & Co Ltd

1	Nelson's flagship Foudroyant		L	C	1/2
2	HMS 'Victory' Flying Nelson's famous signal		L	C	1

SIEFERT, JRH

1	Barbados, Souvenir of Trafalgar	73082	P	C	5

SINCLAIR, CE

1	Trafalgar. The Victory entering Action, October 21st 1805		P	C	4

SMITH, G

1	Nelson's Monument, October 21st 1905		P	B	5

SMITH, SYDNEY

1	HMS Victory Dressed in honor (sic) of HM Queen Victoria's birthday		L	S	2

	KEY				
	Publisher details		**Postcard Details - Legend**		
Item No.	Postcard Caption	Card No.	Landscape Portrait	Colour Black & White Sepia	Value **1** Upto £2.50 **2** £2.60 - £5.50 **3** £5.60 - £12.50 **4** £12.60 - £25.50 **5** £25.60 plus

SMITH, WH & Son - including Derwent Real Photo Series and Sepia Gloss Series

1	HMS Victory	S17925-35	P	B	1
2	HMS Victory Showing Nelson's Famous Signal "England Expects..."		L	S	2

SMITH, WS

1	The Victory - 'England Expects...' (picture of a large mock-up)		P	B	2

SOCIETY FOR NAUTICAL RESEARCH

1	The Victory Museum - Ground Floor		L	C	3
2	The Victory Museum - The Gallery		L	C	3

SOUTHWOOD

1	(Newspaper Facsimile)		P	B	4

STANDARD PICTORIAL POSTCARD Co

1	Portsmouth, HMS Victory	928	P	C	1

STAR SERIES listed under Gottschalk, Dreyfuss & Davis

STENGEL & Co

1	The 'Victory' - Portsmouth Harbour		L	B	1/2

STEPHENSON - Art Series

1	Nelson's Foudroyant at Anchor off Blackpool		L	B	4
2	"The Dying Monarch" Nelson's flagship 'Foudroyant' off Blackpool		L	B	4

STIEBEL, A - including Alpha, Alphalpha and Patriotic Series

1	Nelson's prayer	4258	L	C	2/3

STODDART & Co - including Ja-Ja Heraldic Series

1	Nelson		P	C	2

STONE, B & Sons

1	Untitled (Manuscript inscription "An old anchor believed to have come from one of Nelson's ships RNMDSF Gorleston")		P	B	3/4

STUART, FGO

1	HMS 'Victory' Trafalgar's Day	48812 1367	L	C	1/2
2	HMS Victory. Where Nelson Fell	131967	L	B	1

STUDIO D - issued for Blackpool Centenary 1876-1976

1	Lord Nelson's Flagship, The Foudroyant wrecked on Blackpool Beach 16th June 1897 Modern		L	S	1

E. T. & Co, Wimbledon

1	Nelson's house, Merton		L	C	2/3

TAYLOR, A & G - Reality Series

1	Nelson Centenary. Twas in Trafalgar Bay ... (includes picture after Abbott)		P	B	3
2	Nelson Centenary. England expects that every ... (includes picture after Abbott)		P	B	3

TAYLOR, Will F

1	Greenwich Hospital. The Nelson Relics		L	B	2

Item No.	Postcard Caption	Card No.	Landscape Portrait	Colour Black & White Sepia	Value
	Publisher details		**Postcard Details - Legend**		1 Upto £2.50 2 £2.60 - £5.50 3 £5.60 - £12.50 4 £12.60 - £25.50 5 £25.60 plus

TIFFANY DESIGNS (repros. of paintings by Peter Power 1986)

Item No.	Postcard Caption	Card No.	L/P	C/B/S	Value
1	"Trafalgar: 'Victory' breaking the line" Modern		L	C	1
2	"Trafalgar: 'Santissima Trinidad' reduced" Modern		L	C	1

TOOMBS, JENNIFER

Item No.	Postcard Caption	Card No.	L/P	C/B/S	Value
1	Nelson Museum, Nevis, W Indies Modern		L	C	1

TUCK, R & Sons - including Oilette Series

Item No.	Postcard Caption	Card No.	L/P	C/B/S	Value
1	HMS Victory flying the famous signal, and Submarine B1 (Framed Gem Glosso - Portsmouth)	747	L	C	1
2	HMS Victory. Portsmouth Harbour. Flying Nelson's Famous Signal ...	783	L	C	1
3	Lady Hamilton at the Spinning Wheel (after Romney)	2650	P	C	3
4	HMS 'Victory', Portsmouth	4007	P	C	1/2
5	Nelson Room, Three Cups Hotel, Harwich	4913	L	C	3
6	"England! What thou wert, thou art!" (A Hundred Years Ago - Nelson)	8719	P	C	2
7	As In The Days Of Old! (painting by Prof Albert W Holden, picture as no. 6 above)		P	C	4
8	Nelson's last message (painted by HS Stanley Clarke)	9108	P	C	2
9	The Old and the New. Nelson's Victory and the Latest Submarine (Our Ironclads Series IV)	9109	L	C	2
10	HMS Victory Launched 1765; 2164 tons; flagship stationed at Portsmouth		P	S	2
11	Nelson Collection Monmouth: Chair from HMS Victory		L	S	2
12	Nelson Collection Monmouth: Picture of Lady Hamilton, Telescopes, etc.)		L	S	2
13	Nelson Collection Monmouth: Lady Hamilton by Romney, Wearing Apparel of ...		L	S	2
14	Nelson Collection Monmouth: Presentation Plate, Trophy. Canopy of Spade Guineas		P	S	2
15	The 'Lord Nelson' Burnham Thorpe Norfolk		L	B	3
16	The Nelson Column, Trafalgar Square. Decorated by the Navy League on Trafalgar Day		P	B	2/3
17	HMS 'Victory' (Empire - 'The Empire's Navy' Series 47)	254	P	C	4
18	HMS 'Victory' (Empire - 'Our Navy' Series 598)		P	S	2
19	HMS Victory, Portsmouth Harbour. Flying Nelson's famous signal: England Expects every man to do his duty (View Series 783- Portsmouth)		L	C	1
20	Trafalgar Square and Lord Nelson (painted by Helen McKie) (London Character Series)		P	C	2
21	Horatio, Viscount Nelson 1758-1805 (Our Navy Series)		P	S	1/2
22	Britain's famous seadogs: Viscount Nelson (Artistic Series 832)		P	B	2
23	Battle of St. Vincent, February 14th 1797 (Nelson Centenary Series/Nelson's Famous Victories 6692)		L	C	2
24	Nelson's reception at Naples after the Battle of the Nile August 1798		L	C	2
25	The Battle of Copenhagen, April 1801		L	C	2
26	'Twas in Trafalgar's Bay Oct 21st 1805		L	C	2
27	The Battle of Trafalgar October 21st 1805		L	C	2
28	Nelson's old flagship 'The Victory' in Portsmouth Harbour		L	C	2
	Numbers 29-34 in Raphael Tuck's 'Eventful Nelson Incidents' Series 9137 painted by Robt. H Smith:				
29	Midshipman Nelson lost in Chatham Dockyard		P	C	3
30	Nelson's encounter with a Polar Bear		L	C	2
31	Nelson loses his right eye		P	C	2
32	Nelson's humanity at the Battle of the Nile		L	C	2
33	Nelson's blind eye at Copenhagen		L	C	2
34	The Death of Nelson at Trafalgar 1805		L	C	2
35	"'Twas in Trafalgar Bay October 21st 1805" (from a drawing by Charles J de Lacy) (Deeds of British Heroism Series 9132)		L	C	2/3
36	The Battle of Trafalgar (Clarkson Stanfield RA) (National Gallery Series)	1329	L	S	1
37	Emma Hamilton after Romney		P	C	1/2
38	Lord Nelson's Inkstand... (Real Photograph Series 5178)		L	B	3
39	Viscount Horatio Nelson (Connoisseur Postcard Series 2531 Britain's Famous Sea Dogs 'Born 1758 Viscount Horatio Nelson Died 1805')	2531	P	S	2
40	A call to arms! England expects every man to woo his beauty (A Call To Arms Series III)	8775	P	C	2
41	England expects that every man will do his duty. HMS Victory 2,164 Tons (Empire Postcard Series)	254	P	C	2
42	Portsmouth. Lord Nelson's Flagship HMS Victory (Silverette Series)	1975	L	B	1
43	Southsea. HMS Victory (Flying Nelson's Famous Signal) and submarine B1 (Portsmouth and Southsea 4792)		L	C	2
44	Portsmouth. HMS Victory (flying the famous signal) and submarine B1 (Portsmouth Series 5786)		L	C	2

TUSSAUD, Madam

Item No.	Postcard Caption	Card No.	L/P	C/B/S	Value
1	The Death of Nelson (Titled on right side)	46,509	L	C	1/2
2	The Death of Nelson (Titled on left side)		L	C	1/2

KEY						
Publisher details				**Postcard Details - Legend**		
Item No.	Postcard Caption		Card No.	Landscape Portrait	Colour Black & White Sepia	Value **1** Upto £2.50 **2** £2.60 - £5.50 **3** £5.60 - £12.50 **4** £12.60 - £25.50 **5** £25.60 plus
3	The Battle of Trafalgar ... as it happened. The guns and their crews in action - lower deck	Modern		L	C	1
4	The Battle of Trafalgar ... as it happened. The crew of a gun ready to fire at Trafalgar	Modern		L	C	1
5	The Battle of Trafalgar ... as it happened. The dying but victorious Nelson in the cockpit	Modern		L	C	1
6	The Battle of Trafalgar ... as it happened. Portrait of mortally wounded Nelson	Modern		P	C	1

VALENTINE, J (JV)

1	London. Nelson's Column, Trafalgar Square, Oct 21st 1905. Centenary Battle of Trafalgar			P	B	2/3
2	England Expects That Every Man ... HMS Iron Duke, HMS Victory			P	B	2/3
3	England Expects That Every Man ... HMS Iron Duke, HMS Victory			P	C	1/2
4	London, Nelson's Column, Trafalgar Square Oct 21st 1905		50253	P	B	2/3
5	HMS Victory, Portsmouth (at least three variations of caption/number position)		19212	L	S	1
6	HMS 'Victory' in Portsmouth Dockyard, Southsea (Bromotype)		202819	L	B	2
7	HMS 'Victory', Portsmouth		205266	L	B	1
8	HMS 'Victory', Portsmouth (Valesque)		205266	L	C	1
9	HMS "Victory" Portsmouth Dockyard (49)		205270	L	S	1
10	The Quarter Deck (showing spot where Nelson fell ....)		205273	L	S	1
11	HMS Victory (5 views)		218414	L	S	1
12	The Victory, Portsmouth		K1293	L	B	1
13	The Victory, Portsmouth		K2196	L	C	1
14	Buying War Bonds at the Tank, Trafalgar Square, London			L	B	3
15	Nelson's Prayer Before the Battle of Trafalgar (Helpful thoughts Series)			P	C	2
16	HMS 'Victory', Portsmouth			L	C	1
17	England Expects That Every Man Will Do His Duty			P	B	1
18	England Expects That Every Man Will Do His Duty			P	C	1
19	Types of the British Navy 'Victory', Built 1765			P	C	1/2
20	Buying War Bonds At The Tank In Trafalgar Square, London (Tank 130 'Nelson')			L	B	2/3

VELDALE

1	Maritime Heritage		CBS 15/1	P	C	1

VICTORIA & ALBERT MUSEUM

1	Leonard William Collman Design for Memorial to Nelson	Modern	8595.S	L	B	1/2

VICTORY MUSEUM - including Nelsonian Collection

1	Lord Nelson's Prayer before Trafalgar			P	C	1
2	"Nelson's fatal wound" by Fred J Proctor			L	S	2

VINCENT GRAPHICS

1	Hero of Trafalgar by William Heysman Overend RA 1851-1898	Modern		L	C	1
2	Vice-Admiral Lord Viscount Nelson after Lemuel Abbott	Modern		P	C	1
3	Viscount Nelson as Vice Admiral of the Blue (1801) by John Hoppner RA	Modern		P	C	1
4	Lord Nelson with Lady Hamilton and Horatia (by permission of Royal Naval Museum, Portsmouth)	Modern		L	C	1
5	Return to Harbour by John Ward			L	C	1

WALKER, John & Co Ltd - including Bell's Series

1	Nelson's 'Victory'. The Spot Where Nelson Fell (RP, features George V?)			P	S	2
2	The 'Naiad' towing the 'Belleisle' after Trafalgar		3081	L	S	3

WALKER ART GALLERY

1	The Death of Nelson (detail) by Daniel Maclise 1806-1870	Modern		L	C	1

WALMER CASTLE SERIES

1	Drawing room showing Ante-room in which Nelson and Pitt conferred prior to Trafalgar			L	B	3

WALSHAM'S Ltd

1	Trafalgar Day 1917 Wreath sent by HMS Conqueror			L	S	3

KEY					
Publisher details				**Postcard Details - Legend**	
Item No.	Postcard Caption	Card No.	Landscape Portrait	Colour Black & White Sepia	Value 1 Upto £2.50 2 £2.60 - £5.50 3 £5.60 - £12.50 4 £12.60 - £25.50 5 £25.60 plus

W.E.B. FAVOURITE SERIES listed under Byers, WE

WELCH, J, & Sons

1	The Ajax. The Santissima Trinidad. The Bucenture. The Victory. The Redoubtable. The Victory breaks. The moment of Nelson's death	18	L	C	3
2	The first shot at the Battle of Trafalgar	22	P	C	2
3	England expects that this day every man will do his duty, HMS Victor		L	C	1
4	Nelson's Flagship 'Victory' saluting the King	JWS21	L	B	2
5	Nelson's Ship 'Victory'	6	L	B	1
6	Nelson's Ship 'Victory' (early, undivided back)		L	B	2
7	Nelson's Ship 'Victory' Portsmouth Harbour	6	L	S	1
8	Nelson's ship 'Victory' firing a salute	6	L	B	1
9	HMS Victory, Portsmouth Harbour	18 7514	L	S	1
10	Nelson's ship 'Victory' celebrating Trafalgar Day	22	L	S	1
11	Nelson's Victory Firing a Salute in Portsmouth Harbour		P	C	1
12	Portsmouth Harbour with HMS Victory		L	C	2

WELLINGTON MUSEUM

1	The Army and the Navy from engraving by SW Reynolds after JP Knight RA (picture of Nelson and Wellington) Modern	AP40 E2976-1962	P	C	1
2	Horatio, Viscount Nelson (after Beechey) Modern	AP65	P	C	1

WHITE, GILBERT

1	Bust of Lord Nelson, BurnhamThorpe Church	GW25	P	B	1
2	Burnham Thorpe Church	GW26	L	B	1

WHITE, Timothy & Co Ltd

1	HMS Victory, Portsmouth Harbour (Gordon Series)		L	C	1

WHITE STAR LINE - 'BULWARK'

1	HMS Royal Sovereign - Collingwood's Flagship 1805		L	C	2/3

WILDT & KRAY

1	England expects... (also words from Battle of the Baltic)	3255	P	C	3
2	England expects... (with three oval photo inserts of Churchill, Nelson and Jellicoe?)	3257	L	C	3/4
3	Britannia's Sons Will Guard The Empire...And The Free		P	C	3
4	The Flag That's Burned a Thousand Years - The Battle and the Breeze	3261	L	C	3

WINTERS

1	All Saints Church, Burnham Thorpe (viewed from near the new graveyard)		L	C	1
2	All Saints Church, Burnham Thorpe (Navy Ensign flying from tower)		L	C	1
3	Inn Sign and Church, Burnham Thorpe		P	C	1

WOOLSTONE Bros (also see Keliher and Giesen)

1	HMS Victory Flying Nelson's Signal ('Artlette-Glazette' Series No. 238)		L	C	1
2	Portsmouth HMS Victory		P	C	1
3	HMS Victory, Portsmouth (Milton 'Fac-Simile Sunset' Series No. 248)		P	C	1
4	Portsmouth HMS Victory		P	C	1
	* Postcards in the 'Milton' series 560 are listed under Keliher JJ				

WRENCH

1	Lady Hamilton by G Romney, National Portrait Gallery	75	P	B	2
2	HMS Victory, Portsmouth	348	L	B	1/2
3	HMS Victory, Portsmouth	348	L	C	1/2
4	Lady Hamilton by George Romney (National Gallery)	840	P	S	2
5	HMS 'Victory'	2363	L	B	1
6	Lord Nelson (after Abbott)	10498	P	B	1/2
7	Nelson volunteering to board a privateer in a gale	10499	P	B	1/2
8	The Battle of the Nile	10500	P	B	1
9	Battle of Trafalgar	10501	L	S	1
10	Death of Nelson in the cockpit of the Victory	10502	L	B	1

Item No.	Postcard Caption	Card No.	Landscape Portrait	Colour Black & White Sepia	Value 1 Upto £2.50 2 £2.60 - £5.50 3 £5.60 - £12.50 4 £12.60 - £25.50 5 £25.60 plus
	Publisher details			**Postcard Details - Legend**	

| 11 | The Font, Burnham Thorpe Church | 14191 | P | C | 2 |
| 12 | Nelson's Brook, Burnham Thorpe | 14192 | P | C | 2 |

WRIGHT & LOGAN (some black & white cards are also found in sepia)

No.	Caption		L/P	Colour	Value
1	'Leviathan' (British) 'Santissima Trinidad' (Spanish) 'Neptune' (British) and 'Africa' (British)		L	B	2/3
2	'Fougeux' (French) 'Temeraire' (British) 'Redoubtable' (French) 'Victory' (Lord Nelson's flagship)		L	B	2/3
3	Vice-Admiral Collingwood's Flagship 'Royal Sovereign' and Spanish ship 'Santa Ana'		L	S	2/3
4	State barge of King Charles II which conveyed Nelson's body to Whitehall		L	S	2/3
5	Nelson's dining room - showing original furniture - HMS Victory		L	B	1
6	Nelson's dining room, showing original furniture		L	S	1
7	Nelson's dining room, showing original furniture		L	B	1
8	Tablet on board HMS 'Victory' marking spot where Nelson fell		L	S	1
9	Where Nelson died, HMS Victory		L	S	1
10	Where Nelson died - similar scene, different picture detail to 8 above		L	S	1
11	Where Nelson fell		L	S	1
12	Quarterdeck, Looking Forward, HMS Victory		L	S	1
13	Quarterdeck, looking forward		L	S	1
14	HMS Victory, Nelson's Flagship, The Shrine of the Navy		P	S	1/2
15	HMS Victory		L	S	1
16	HMS Victory under sail		L	S	1/2
17	Figurehead HMS 'Victory'		L	S	1
18	Figurehead. HMS Victory		P	S	1
19	Quarterdeck, looking aft		L	S	1
20	HMS Victory (dressed with flags)		L	S	1
21	HMS Victory Flying Nelson's Famous Signal (inset of Nelson)		P	S	1
22	Victory II		L	S	2
23	Six Views of HMS Victory. Real Photographic. (Set of six cards in packet)				2

YALLOP, AW

No.	Caption		L/P	Colour	Value
1	The Nelson Centenary 1805-1905. Celebrations At Great Yarmouth…20 Oct 1905		L	B	4/5
2	Nelson Room 'Star Hotel', Yarmouth. Proprietor: H Taylor		L	B	2

YARDLEY, ALICE C

No.	Caption		L/P	Colour	Value
1	Nelson landing at Yarmouth, November 6, 1800		L	S	3

UNIDENTIFIED PUBLISHERS

A. Pictorial Post Card.

No.	Caption		L/P	Colour	Value
	It is probable that these postcards were published by JJ Coleman of Norwich, but this has not been definitely established. They were published in both standard and reduced size, and nos. 1-13 are found with gold border.				
1	The Star Hotel, Great Yarmouth, as it appeared in the time of Nelson, who often stayed there		P	C	2
2	Nelson leaves home to go to sea for the first time, 1771		P	C	1
3	Nelson at twelve years of age waiting to embark on board the 'Raissonable' of sixty-four guns. AD 1771		P	C	1
4	Battle of St Vincent Feb 14th 1797. Nelson receiving the dying Spanish Admiral's sword, now in the Guildhall Norwich		P	C	1
5	Battle of St Vincent AD 1797. Nelson embraced by his superior officer Admiral Jervis in gratitude and admiration after the battle		P	C	2
6	Nelson loses his arm in the night attack on the Mole at Santa Cruz. AD 1797 (also seen with gold scroll behind writing)		P	C	2
7	Nelson presented with the Freedom of the City of London and Gold Casket of 100 guineas value. Chamberlain's Office, Guildhall, Nov 1797		P	C	2
8	Nelson at Copenhagen 1801		P	C	2
9	Battle of Copenhagen. Nelson holding the Telescope to his blind eye says he cannot see Admiral Parker's signal to retreat April 1801		P	C	1/2
10	Nelson arranging his famous signal before the Battle of Trafalgar, Oct 21st 1805		P	C	2
11	The Battle of Trafalgar, Oct 21st 1805		L	C	1
12	Battle of Trafalgar. Nelson receives his death wound. Oct 1805		P	C	2
13	Death of Nelson in the Cockpit of the 'Victory' Oct 21st 1805		L	C	2
14	Nelson 1801		P	C	2
15	Burnham Thorpe Old Rectory, Nelson's First Home		L	C	1

	Publisher details		Postcard Details - Legend		
Item No.	Postcard Caption	Card No.	Landscape Portrait	Colour Black & White Sepia	Value **1** Upto £2.50 **2** £2.60 - £5.50 **3** £5.60 - £12.50 **4** £12.60 - £25.50 **5** £25.60 plus
16	Norwich Grammar School (of which Nelson was a scholar) 'Nelson's statue' near by		L	C	1
17	Nelson leaving for Trafalgar		L	C	3
18	Nelson attacks a Spanish Launch, July 3rd 1797 from a Picture by R Westall RA		P	C	1/2
19	Nelson's famous signal before the Battle of Trafalgar		P	C	2/3
20	Part of the first letter written by Nelson after the loss of his right arm		L	C	2

B. Other

Item No.	Postcard Caption	Card No.	Landscape Portrait	Colour Black & White Sepia	Value
1	HMS Victory. Best Wisches (sic) (Silk) (His Majesty's Ships Series)		L	C	5
2	Nelson	108	P	S	2
3	Portrait of Lady Hamilton (after Romney)	494	P	C	2
4	The original marriage certificate of Lord Nelson (Nevis W Indies)		L	B	3
5	The Old Rectory, Burnham Thorpe, Nelson's birthplace		L	B	1
6	Burnham Thorpe Rectory, Nelson's birthplace (shows existing building. RP)		L	B	3/4
7	Nelsons Inn, Burnham Thorpe. Where Nelson gave a farewell dinner before his last voyage	94528	L	B	5
8	Nelson's Old House, Burnham Thorpe. Where he gave a farewell dinner before his last voyage (same RP as above)	94528	L	B	5
9	Burnham Thorpe Church. The Font Where Nelson was christened	94529	P	B	2
10	Nelson		P	B	2
11	Handwritten inscription ... 'Nelson's Church, Burnham Thorpe from NE'		L	S	3
12	Handwritten inscription ... 'Site of Nelson's birth place with the Old Pump, Burnham Thorpe'		L	S	4
13	Handwritten inscription ... 'Interior - The Church Burnham Thorpe (Nelson's Birthplace)'		P	S	3
14	The 'Lord Nelson', Burnham Thorpe, Norfolk		L	B	1
15	Bucklers Hard. Where the 'Agamemnon' was built	83	L	B	3
16	Burnham Thorpe Church		L	B	1/2
17	Burnham Thorpe Church		L	S	1
18	The Old Rectory, Burnham Thorpe 'Nelson's Birthplace'		L	B	1
19	Nelson's last farewell to England		L	S	2
20	Nelson's famous signal before the Battle of Trafalgar (undivided back)		P	C	2
21	Lord Nelson's signal at Trafalgar (flags, code nos.)		P	C	2/3
22	Nelson's signal		P	C	2/3
23	Nelson wounded		L	S	2/3
24	Lord Nelson mortally wounded Oct 21 1805		P	C	2/3
25	Nelson's prayer on the eve of Trafalgar		P	S	3
26	Death of Nelson on board the Victory (after B West RA)		L	B	2
27	Nelson	64	P	S	1
28	Death of Nelson	65	L	S	2
29	Victory leaving Portsmouth	66	P	S	1
30	HMS Victory off Cadiz	67	L	S	1/2
31	HMS Victory 1805	68	P	S	1/2
32	Nelson wounded	69	L	S	2
33	After Trafalgar	330	L	S	2
34	Death of Nelson (after B West)	4352	L	B	2
35	HMS 'Victory', Portsmouth	4527	P	S	1
36	Nelson at prayer in his cabin before the Battle of Trafalgar	5510	P	B	3
37	Nelson's Monument Oct 21st 1905		P	S	4
38	Trafalgar 1805-1905 - HMS Victory, Nelson's signal and Nelson		L	C	3
39	Broad Str. Trafalgar Day 21st Oct 1905 - Barbados		P	B	4
40	County Borough of Great Yarmouth Nelson Centenary 1905		P	C	3
41	Trafalgar Centenary Oct 21st 1805 1905		L	B	3
42	Trafalgar Centenary Horatio Nelson		P	C	2/3
43	Church Kirk Oct 22/05 - Nelson Centenary at Church Kirk		L	S	3/4
44	1805 1905. Nelson's dying words, 21st October, 1805: "Thank God…"		L	C	2/3
45	1805 "England Expects" 1905….Are You Doing Your Duty Today? - Affiches De La Grande Guerre No 15		L	C	2/3
46	The Death of Nelson in the Cockpit of the 'Victory', 1805 by G Devas		L	S	2
47	Untitled (Picture of Nelson's bust in All Saints Church, Burnham Thorpe)		P	B	2
48	PS Lord Nelson, Yarmouth (Paddle Steamer)		L	B	2
49	Lord Nelson, Westminster Abbey		P	S	1/2
50	HMS Victory, Nelson's room at the George Hotel, The Victory's Cockpit - B & B Series		L	C	1/2
51	Allegorical carving "The Death of Nelson" carved by a sailor 1806		L	B	1/2
52	Tablet inserted in wall of George Hotel Portsmouth		P	B	2/3
53	Bust of Viscount Nelson		P	B	2/3
54	Death of Nelson (includes lines of music by Braham)		L	C	3
55	Death of Nelson (includes lines of music - Along the line the signal ran. Also seen without ref. no...)	18/3A	P	C	3

	KEY				
	Publisher details		**Postcard Details - Legend**		
Item No.	Postcard Caption	Card No.	Landscape Portrait	Colour Black & White Sepia	Value **1** Upto £2.50 **2** £2.60 - £5.50 **3** £5.60 - £12.50 **4** £12.60 - £25.50 **5** £25.60 plus
56	Three Cheers for the Red, White and Blue	485-1	L	C	2
57	Rule Britannia	485-4	L	C	2
58	Send Him Victorious	485-5	L	C	2
59	Invasion of England Now Boys Down With Nelson the first thing (sic)	73	L	S	3
60	Photo of Original Bust (by Sir Edgar Boehm)on top of the 'Nelson' Column, Portsdown Hill	974	P	S	5
61	Nelson's Memorial Tablet, Jamaica, British West Indies	25242	P	C	2/3
62	Trafalgar Square showing Nelson's Statue Barbados	48760-B	L	C	2
63	The Cathedral of the Navy. HMS Victory, Showing Stern . Tonnage 2162 Tons		L	S	1
64	HMS Victory (four small pictures) Modern	PLC2644	L	C	1
65	HMS Victory July 1928 Middle Deck & Officers Quarters	17172	L	S	2
66	'The Victory' Flying Nelson's Famous Signal, Portsmouth	4	P	S	1
67	Nelson's ship 'Victory' firing a salute	6	P	S	2
68	HMS Victory in Portsmouth Dockyard		L	S	1
69	HMS Victory	25	P	B	1
70	HMS Victory, Portsmouth. Reconstructed July, 1928	26	P	B	1
71	HMS Victory, Portsmouth. Reconstructed July, 1928	26	P	C	1
72	Figurehead of HMS Victory. Built 1765		P	B	2
73	Figurehead of 'Lord Nelson' Built 1860		P	B	4
74	II. England: 'Victory', Portsmouth		L	C	2
75	Anchor of HMS Victory		L	C	1
76	'The Victory' flying Nelson's Famous Signal. Portsmouth	12	P	B	1
77	'The Victory' flying Nelson's Famous Signal. Portsmouth		P	C	1
78	HMS 'Victory'. Portsmouth. (Reconstructed July 1928)		P	S	1
79	HMS 'Victory'		L	S	1
80	HMS Victory 5 vignettes (Excel Series)	68	L	S	1
81	HMS Victory 5 vignettes (Excel Series)	68A	L	B	1
82	HMS Victory 5 vignettes - different (Excel Series)	68	L	S	1
83	HMS Victory Portsmouth (Souvenir Viewcard from the drawing by John Mortlock)		L	C	2
84	HMS Victory, Portsmouth Harbour		L	B	1
85	HMS Victory s. 213/212 (prob. Misch & Co.)	36125	P	C	1
86	The 'Victory'. Portsmouth Harbour (FCC)		L	S	1
87	HMS Victory (dressed for Trafalgar Day)		P	B	1
88	HMS 'Victory' Portsmouth	41	P	S	1
89	Victory Flying Nelson's Famous Signal	21	P	S	1
90	HMS 'Victory'. Portsmouth	W4075	L	B	1
91	HMS Victory (Wyndham Series)	W8280	L	B	1
92	HMS Victory from Gosport (CAP Series)		L	B	1
93	HMS Victory Portsmouth		L	S	1
94	HMS Victory, Portsmouth (Spithead Series)	613	L	C	1
95	HMS Victory	9422	L	B	1
96	HMS Victory (Raleigh Series)	25	P	B	1
97	Lord Nelson (portrait in blue ink after Chas. Lucy painting)		P	C	3
98	Wreck of Foudroyant at Blackpool	BT 44	L	B	4
99	George Hotel, High St, Portsmouth. It was here Lord Nelson spent his last hours in England Sep 14, 1805		L	B	3
100	Nelson's Statue, 21st Oct. 1905, Barbados		L	S	3/4
101	Lord Nelson's Flagship 'HMS Victory'. Tablet inserted in Wall of George Hotel Portsmouth		P	C	3/4
102	England's Honour ... (Speech extract) ... Lord Nelson in the House of Lords ...		P	C	3
103	Model of HMS Victory constructed from Studiette Galleon Kit no.2905(Trade card)		L	B	2
104	HMS Boscawen 1841-1905 (Figurehead of Nelson originally from HMS Trafalgar renamed HMS Boscawen in 1873)		P	S	3/4
105	Untitled (Figurehead of Nelson from HMS Vanguard 1835)		P	B	3/4
106	Souvenir of the Nelson Centenary 1805-1905 (with additional verse to the *Death of Nelson*. Similar in concept to the P Jones card but different in design)		L	C	3/4
107	Hearts of Oak (with verse ... Come, cheer up lads, 'tis to glory we steer,)		P	C	2
108	The 'Implacable' ... the only ship still afloat which fought at Trafalgar .(Fund raising card for The Society for Nautical Research, National Maritime Museum ... includes picture of Foudroyant, 103mm x 150mm)		L	B	3
109	Trafalgar Square - Barbados		L	S	2/3
110	Lord Nelson's Flagship HMS Victory. Portsmouth (during restoration)		P	S	2
111	Nelson's Centenary on Trafalgar Square		L	B	3
112	'Here Nelson Fell' ('Our Navy')		L	B	1/2
113	Navy Week, Chatham. HMS Victory No. 1(Victory II at sea)		P	B	2/3
114	HMS Boscawen Figure-Head Shotley Barracks		P	S	2
115	Shade of Nelson:- "Well Done Jack, You're The Same Old Stuff"	W617	P	S	1
116	(handwritten note: 'One of Nelson's ships. This one used as a training ship for cadets')		L	S	4